Documents and Debates
Seventeenth—Century Britain

Documents and Debates
General Editor: John Wroughton M.A., F.R.Hist.S.

Seventeenth-Century Britain

John Wroughton, F. R. Hist. S.

Headmaster, King Edward's School, Bath

Macmillan Education
London and Basingtoke

First published 1980
Reprinted 1981, 1982, 1983

Published by
MACMILLAN EDUCATION LIMITED
Houndmills Basingstoke Hampshire RG21 2XS
and London
Associated companies in Delhi   Dublin
Hong Kong   Johannesburg   Lagos   Melbourne
New York   Singapore and Tokyo

Printed in Hong Kong

British Library Cataloguing in Publication Data
Wroughton, John
Seventeenth century Britain. — (Documents and debates).
1. Great Britain — History — Stuarts, 1603—1714
I. Title   II. Series
941.06   DA375
ISBN 0-333-24572-5

Contents

General Editor's Preface

This book forms part of a series entitled *Documents and Debates*, which is aimed primarily at the sixth form. Each volume covers approximately one century of either British or European history and consists of up to ten sections, each dealing with a major theme. In most cases a varied selection of documents will bring evidence to bear on the chosen theme, supplemented by a stimulating extract from a modern historian. A few 'Debate' sections, however, will centre on the most important controversies of each century. Here extracts from the changing opinions of modern research, normally found only in learned journals and expensive monographs, will be made available in manageable form. The series intends partly to provide experience for those pupils who are required to answer questions on documentary extracts at 'A' Level, and partly to provide pupils of all abilities with a digestible and interesting collection of source material, which will extend the normal textbook approach.

This book is designed essentially for the pupil's own personal use. The author's introduction will put the century as a whole into perspective, highlighting the central issues, main controversies, available source material and recent developments. Although it is clearly not our intention to replace the traditional textbook, each section will carry its own brief introduction, which will set the documents into context. The short, select bibliography is intended to encourage the pupil to follow up issues raised in the section by further reading – without being subjected to the off-putting experience of an exhaustive list. A wide variety of source material has been used in order to give the pupils the maximum amount of experience – letters, speeches, newspapers, memoirs, diaries, official papers, Acts of Parliament, Minute Books, accounts, local documents, family papers etc. The questions vary in difficulty, but aim throughout to compel the pupil to think in depth by the use of unfamiliar material. Historical knowledge and understanding will be tested, as well as basic comprehension. Pupils will also be encouraged by the questions to assess the reliability of evidence, to recognise bias and emotional prejudice, to reconcile conflicting accounts and to extract the essential from the irrelevant. Some questions, marked with an asterisk, require knowledge outside the immediate extract and are intended for further research or discussion, based on the pupil's general knowledge of the period. Finally, we hope that students using this material will learn something of the nature of historical inquiry and the role of the historian.

John Wroughton

Acknowledgements

The author and publishers wish to thank the following who have kindly given permission for the use of copyright material:-

Associated Book Publishers Ltd for extracts from *England Under the Stuarts* by G. M. Trevelyan, published by Methuen & Co. Ltd and *Oliver Cromwell's Letters and Speeches (1845)* by Thomas Carlyle, published by Chapman & Hall Ltd

Avebury Publishing Company Ltd for extracts from *Historical Collections of Private Passages of State . . . . . .* London 1659–1701 8 Vols; by John Rushworth;

Bath City Council for extracts from *Bath Chamberlains Accounts, 1643–1645* and *Bath Council Minute Book 1643–1646*;

Cambridge University Press for an extract from *The Rump Parliament 1648–1653* by Brian Worden;

The Controller of Her Majesty's Stationery Office for extracts from *Bill of Rights 1689* and *Corporation Act 1661*;

J. M. Dent & Sons Ltd for extracts from *Memoirs of the Life of Colonel Hutchinson* reproduced in Everyman Library Series;

Gerald Duckworth & Co. Ltd for an extract from *Oliver Cromwell* by C. V. Wedgwood;

Encounter Ltd for extracts from *Storm Over the Gentry* by J. H. Hexter;

The Historical Association for extracts from *The Local Community and the Great Rebellion* by A. M. Everitt, and *The Stuarts* by K. H. D. Haley;

Thomas Nelson & Sons Ltd for extracts from *Century of Revolution* by Christopher Hill;

Oxford University Press for extracts from *History of the Rebellion* by Clarendon; *Memoirs of Edmund Ludlow* edited by C. M. Firth, and *Oliver Cromwell and the Rule of the Puritans in England* by C. M. Firth;

Oxford University Press for an extract from *Pride's Purge* by David Underdown;

A. D. Peters & Co. Ltd on behalf of Sir Arthur Bryant for an extract from *King Charles II*;

Routledge & Keegan Paul Ltd for extracts from *Diaries and Letters of Phillip Henry* edited by M. M. Lee, and *The Puritan Revolution* edited by S. E. Prall;

Martin Secker & Warburg Ltd for extracts from *Puritanism and Revolution* by Christopher Hill;

Professor Hugh Trevor-Roper and the Economic History Review for an extract from *The Gentry, 1540–1640*, Economic History Review, Supplement No. 1 (1953).

The University of Chicago Press for an extract from David Hume, *History of England*, Vol. 8, edited by John Clive;

Professor A. H. Woolrych for extracts from *The Collapse of the Great Rebellion*;

Cover Bodleian Library.

Every effort has been made to trace all the copyright holders but if any have been inadvertently overlooked the publishers will be pleased to make the necessary arrangement at the first opportunity.

The Seventeenth Century

The central theme of the years 1603–89 was undoubtedly the struggle between king and parliament. From the outset, James I's belief in the Divine Right of Kings was challenged by successive parliaments which tirelessly stressed their own privileges and birthrights. The king's *right* to collect impositions, tunnage and poundage and ship money, his *right* to exclusive control of foreign policy and his *right* to appoint his own ministers were effectively denied by parliament in their Petition of Right (1628), Three Resolutions (1629) and Grand Remonstrance (1641). Neither the Civil War, which followed, nor the trial and execution of Charles I really ended this contest for sovereignty. It is true that Charles II, at the Restoration in 1660, returned without a Court of Star Chamber, without a Court of High Commission and without the right to tax at will, but a convincing victory of parliamentary government over absolute monarchy was denied until William and Mary gave royal assent to the Bill of Rights in 1689. This victory was both remarkable and significant. It was achieved very much against the tide. Elsewhere in Europe governments were becoming more despotic and less parliamentarian. The French had to wait another century before their revolution was attempted. It was significant, partly because of the influence it later exerted on other countries, and partly because it laid the foundation for the establishment of parliamentary democracy in nineteenth-century England.

Another main theme, closely allied to the struggle between king and parliament, was that of religion. The Civil War itself was, up to a point at least, an expression of the demand made by puritan sects for 'freedom of conscience'. Temporary respite was indeed achieved during the years of Commonwealth and Protectorate – only to be snatched away by the terms of the Clarendon Code (1661–5). Not until the Toleration Act of 1689 did non-conformists enjoy the right to freedom of worship. Far more significant, however, to the constitutional developments of this century was the ever-present fear of a catholic revival based on the monarchy. This was made evident by widespread public hostility to the proposed Spanish alliance and marriage of Prince Charles to the Spanish Infanta (1623), to Archbishop Laud's 'innovations' in the church (1630s), to the Secret Treaty of Dover (1670), to the 'Popish Plot' (1678) and to the Declaration of Indulgence (1687). The Test Act (1673), the Exclusion Bill (1680), the Rye House Plot (1683) and Monmouth's rebellion (1685) all really carried the same basic message – that Catholics in high places were unwelcome to the people of this country.

Students of the seventeenth century will certainly find an abundant supply of source material at their disposal, much of it now in printed form. Furthermore, the main 'facts' of the story are very well established in fundamental textbooks and chronological date charts. And yet the century has remained one of the most controversial battlegrounds for historians over the last three hundred years. Facts are seldom in dispute. Interpretations are. Memoirs and early histories of the period, written by people who were themselves actors in the plot (Rushworth, Burnet, Hutchinson, Baxter, Ludlow, Clarendon, the Venetian Ambassador, etc.) were invariably coloured by personal passion and prejudice. Reputations needed to be saved, actions to be justified, enemies to be blackened. Later histories too, tended to be regarded as opportunities for party political propaganda, whether in the form of Hume's 'Tory Interpretation' of the period or Macaulay's 'Whig Interpretation'. Students of history would do well to ask questions first about the writer himself, his background, beliefs and motives, before accepting completely his selection, arrangement and interpretation of the facts.

Great strides, however, have been made over the last one hundred and fifty years in our knowledge and understanding of the seventeenth century. This has largely been the result of a number of new ideas and methods which have changed our approach to the study of history. First of all, from the German universities in the middle of the nineteenth century, came 'scientific history', which placed a heavy emphasis on the study of original records. The writings of S. R. Gardiner and C. H. Firth immediately reflected the different approach. Modern students now have immediate access to the main letters, speeches and State Papers of the period in various collections: W. C. Abbott, *Writings and Speeches of Oliver Cromwell*, S. R. Gardiner, *Constitutional Documents of the Puritan Revolution*, J. P. Kenyon, *The Stuart Constitution*, J. Thurloe, *State Papers* etc. Secondly, under the influence of such writers as Karl Marx, there has developed an awareness of the importance of economics in the understanding of historical events. Historians who go in search of the causes of the Civil War now consider economic fluctuations and social structure alongside religious and constitutional issues. One of the best economic and social histories of this period is C. H. Wilson, *England's Apprenticeship 1603–1763*.

Thirdly, in more recent years, two fresh areas of historical investigation have attracted attention. G. E. Aylmer, in two scholarly studies (*The King's Servants; the civil service of Charles I, 1625–1642* and *The State's Servants; the civil service of the Interregnum, 1653–1660*), has focused his interest on 'administrative' history. Meanwhile, A. M. Everitt, Valerie Pearl, David Underdown, Clive Holmes, Roger Howell and others have been examining 'the Local Community and the Great Rebellion'. Old generalisations based on the national narrative have been seriously modified in the face of evidence produced by these local studies. At the same time, research into local documents, family papers, Council Minute Books, etc. has highlighted the feelings, problems and needs of ordinary, anonymous people, whose world was far removed from that of Charles I or even John Pym. Fourthly, the study of psychology has made historians increasingly aware of hidden motives in the pattern of human behaviour, and thus far more questioning in their appraisal of famous characters. Finally, the application of statistical analysis to historical problems has enabled historians like David Underdown and Blair Worden to support their theories with 'hard' evidence (although at times the *use* of statistics has been challenged – see section III, 'The Gentry Controversy').

All these developments in the study of history have inevitably had their effect on the type of history that is being written. Pure narrative is no longer fashionable – although C. V. Wedgwood's excellent books, *The King's Peace 1637–41* and *The King's War, 1641–7*, are still deservedly popular. Histories of the period tend to be less chronological and more analytical, less political and more given to economic causes (e.g. Christopher Hill, *The Century of Revolution, 1603–1714*). The 'Gentry Controversy', which raged amongst historians with unprecedented bitterness, illustrated vividly this new approach (see section III). But whatever the emphasis, the seventeenth century will always remain one of the most exciting, stimulating and profitable periods for study.

I King and Parliament
1603—40

Introduction

The early years of the century witnessed a debate of ever-increasing intensity concerning the lawful powers of king and parliament. Both James I and Charles I at least, believed in the theory of the Divine Right of Kings, which made them answerable for their actions to God in heaven and not to the people in parliament. While accepting in' practice that kings needed to act within the bounds established by the common law, they nevertheless insisted that parliaments met by the grace of the sovereign king himself. Opposing this view were those who felt that kings had originally derived their power from election by the people and that the people remained 'sovereign'. Parliament, while agreeing that the king enjoyed certain prerogatives and the right to rule, nevertheless argued that it too possessed privileges and powers which were 'the ancient and undoubted birth right and inheritance of the subjects of England'. The successful working of the English constitution depended on the maintenance of this fine balance of powers.

The situation, however, was seriously aggravated between 1603 and 1640, partly by the clumsiness of both James I and Charles I in handling their parliaments, and partly by the biting consequences of inflation which made both king and parliament extremely sensitive over money matters. Fundamental issues were raised as each side pressed with growing vehemence its own claims. Did the king's absolute power enable him to collect impositions and ship money – or did this infringe parliament's traditional right to vote all supply? Were matters of foreign policy reserved solely for the decisions of the king – or did parliament have the right to debate any matter of state? Did parliament's freedom of speech extend to criticism of the king's ministers?

Kings did, of course, possess one effective power to cut short the opposition – namely, the dissolution of parliament. Neither James I nor Charles I hesitated to use it. The Personal Rule (1629– 40) was born out of frustration and impatience with truculent parliaments. It ended when Charles I, faced with a Scottish army, conceded that parliament's money-raising power was essential to his government.

Further Reading

John Adair, *A Life of John Hampden, the Patriot* (Macdonald and Jane's, 1976)

S. R. Gardiner, *History of England from the accession of James I to the outbreak of the Civil War* (London, 1883—4)

J. H. Hexter, *The Reign of King Pym* (Cambridge, Mass., 1941)

D. Harris Willson, *King James VI and I* (London, 1956)

1 James I's View of Kingship

The state of monarchy is the supremest thing upon earth; for Kings are not only God's lieutenants upon earth, and sit upon God's throne, but even by God himself they are called gods . . . . Kings are justly called gods; for that they exercise a manner or resemblance of divine power
5 upon earth. For, if you will consider the attributes of God, you shall see how they agree in the person of a King. God hath power to create or destroy, make or unmake, at his pleasure; to give life or send death, to judge all, and not to be judged nor accountable to none; to raise low things, and to make high things low at his pleasure, and to God are both
10 soul and body due. And the like power have Kings; they make and unmake their subjects; they have power of raising and casting down; of life and of death; judges over all their subjects, and in all causes, and yet accountable to none but God only. They have power to exalt low things, and abase high things and make of their subjects like men at the chess; a
15 pawn to take a bishop or a knight, and to cry up or down any of their subjects, as they do their money. And to the King is due both the affection of the soul and the service of the body of his subjects.

Somers Tracts, Vol III, p 260

Questions

a List, in your own words, the ways in which a subject's life could be affected by the king.

* b Explain why James's claim that kings were 'accountable to none but God only' (line 13) was so resented. On which particular occasions did this become an issue between king and parliament during the years 1603—42?

* c Give examples of the way in which James I and Charles I used their power to 'make and unmake their subjects' between 1603 and 1642.

* d What attitude, according to James, can a king adopt to the wealth of his subjects? Illustrate, with examples, the practical implications of this during the reigns of James I and Charles I.

2 The Protestation of the Commons 1621

The Commons now assembled in Parliament ... do make this Protestation following: That the Liberties, Franchises, Privileges, and Jurisdictions of Parliament are the ancient and undoubted Birth right and Inheritance of the subjects of England; and that the arduous and urgent
5 affairs concerning the King, State and Defence of the Realm, and of the Church of England, and the maintenance and making of Laws, and redress of mischiefs and grievances which daily happen within this Realm, are proper subjects and matter of Counsel and Debate in Parliament; and that in the handling and proceeding of those businesses,
10 every Member of the House of Parliament hath, and of right ought to have, freedom of speech to propound, treat, reason and bring to conclusion the same. And that the Commons in Parliament have like liberty and freedom to treat of these matters in such order as in their judgments shall seem fittest. And that every member of the said House
15 hath like freedom from all Impeachment, Imprisonment, and Molestation (otherwise than by Censure of the House itself) for or concerning any speaking, reasoning, or declaring of matters touching the Parliament, or Parliament-business. And that if any of the said members be complained of and questioned for anything done or said in Parliament,
20 the same is to be showed to the King by the advice and assent of all the Commons assembled in Parliament, before the King give credence to any private information.

His Majesty did this present day in full assembly of his Council and in presence of the Judges, declare the said Protestation to be invalid, annulled, void,
25 *and of no effect. And did further* manua sua propria *take the said Protestation out of the Journal Book of the Clerk of the Commons House of Parliament.*
J. Rushworth, *Historical Collections,* 1659, Vol 1, p 53

Questions

a Explain what you understand by 'Liberties, Franchises, Privileges, and Jurisdictions of Parliament' (lines 2 and 3) and by 'Impeachment' (line 15).

b On which topics did parliament feel fully justified in first debating and then offering its advice to the king?

c Which two basic freedoms were claimed by parliament for its members?

* *d* Which 'urgent affairs concerning the King, State and Defence of the Realm' (lines 4 and 5) had parliament been discussing prior to this Protestation in 1621, much to the king's displeasure?

* *e* Explain why James took such strong action against the Protestation (lines 23—6). What consequences immediately followed this outburst in Council?

3   Parliament's Attack on Buckingham 1628

Mr. Alured to Mr. Chamberlain

Sir,

Yesterday was a day of desolation among us in Parliament, and this day we fear will be the day of our dissolution: Upon Tuesday Sir John Eliot moved, that as we intended to furnish his Majesty with money, we should also supply him with Counsel, which was one part of the occasion why
5 we were sent by the Country, and called for by his Majesty: And since that House was the greatest Council of the Kingdom, where, or when should His Majesty have better Council than from thence? So he desired there might be a Declaration made to the King of the danger wherein the Kingdom stood by the decay and contempt of Religion, the insufficiency
10 of his Generals, the unfaithfulness of his Officers, the weakness of his Councils, the exhausting of his Treasure, the death of his men, the decay of Trade, the loss of Shipping, the many and powerful Enemies, the few and poor Friends we had abroad . . . .

So the next day, being Wednesday, we had a Message from his Majesty
15 by the Speaker that the Session should end on Wednesday, and that therefore we should husband the time, and despatch the old businesses without entertaining new . . . . The House was much affected to be so restrained . . . . Then Sir Robert Philips spake, and mingled his words with weeping. Mr. Prynne did the like, and Sir Edward Coke, overcome
20 with passion, seeing the desolation likely to ensue, was forced to sit down when he began to speak, through the abundance of tears . . . . In the end they desired the Speaker to leave the Chair, and Mr. Whitby was to come into it, that they might speak the freer and the frequenter, and commanded that no man go out of the House upon pain of going to the
25 Tower . . . . Then Sir Edward Coke told them . . . he not knowing whether ever he should speak in this House again, would now do it freely, and there protested that the author and cause of all those miseries was the Duke of Buckingham, which was entertained and answered with a cheerful acclamation of the House; . . . and as they were voting it to the
30 question whether they should name him in their intended Remonstrance, the Sole or the Principal cause of all their Miseries at home and abroad; The Speaker having been three hours absent, and with the King, returned with this Message; That the House should then rise till tomorrow morning. What we shall expect this morning God of Heaven knows.

J. Rushworth, *Historical Collections*, 1659, Vol I, p 609

Questions

a What arguments did Eliot use to justify parliament's wish to offer advice to the king?

b For what reasons did Eliot believe that the kingdom was in serious danger?

c What evidence is there here to suggest that the Speaker was more in sympathy with the king? Why was this so?

* d Write briefly on the importance of (i) Sir John Eliot (line 2) (ii) Mr Prynne (line 19) (iii) Sir Edward Coke (line 19) (iv) the Duke of Buckingham (line 28).

* e From your knowledge of the early years of Charles I's reign (1625–8), give examples of (i) 'the insufficiency of his Generals' (lines 9 and 10) (ii) 'the decay and contempt of Religion' (line 9) (iii) 'the many and powerful Enemies' (line 12).

* f Explain why by 1628, (i) the Treasury was exhausted (line 11) (ii) trade was in a state of decay (lines 11 and 12).

4 The Petition of Right 1628

Whereas it is declared and enacted by a statute made in the time of the reign of King Edward I that no tallage or aid shall be laid or levied by the King or his heirs in this realm, without the good will and assent of the archbishops, bishops, earls, barons, knights, burgesses and other the
5 freemen of the commonalty of this realm; and by authority of the Parliament . . . of King Edward III it is decreed and enacted: that from henceforth no person should be compelled to make any loans to the King against his will, because such loans were against reason . . . . Yet nevertheless of late . . . your people have been in divers places assembled,
10 and required to lend certain sums of money unto your Majesty, and (some) of them, upon their refusal so to do . . . have been constrained to become bound to make appearance, and give attendance before your privy council; and others of them have been therefore imprisoned . . . .

And whereas by the Statute called the Great Charter of the Liberties of
15 England, it is declared and enacted, that no freeman may be taken or imprisoned . . . but by the lawful judgment of his peers or by the law of the land . . . . Nevertheless, against the tenour of the said statutes . . . divers of your subjects have of late been imprisoned without any cause shewed. And when for their deliverance they were brought
20 before your justices, by your Majesty's writs of *Habeas Corpus* . . . yet were returned back to several prisons, without being charged with anything to which they might make answer according to law.

And whereas of late great companies of soldiers and mariners have been dispersed into divers counties of the realm; and the inhabitants,
25 against their wills, have been compelled to receive them into their houses, and there to suffer them to sojourn against the laws and customs of this realm, and to the great grievance and vexation of the people . . . .

They do therefore humbly pray your most excellent Majesty that no man hereafter be compelled to make or yield any gift, or loan,
30 benevolence, tax, or such like charge, without common consent by act of parliament. And that none be called to make answer, or to take such oath, or to give attendance, or be confined, or otherwise molested or

disquieted, concerning the same or for refusal thereof. And that no freeman, in any such manner as is before mentioned, be imprisoned or
35 detained. And that your majesty would be pleased to remove the said soldiers and mariners, and that your people may not be so burdened in time to come. And that the foresaid commissioners for proceeding by martial law may be revoked and annulled . . . .

> *Somers Tracts*, Vol IV, p 117

Questions

a What three main grievances against the king did parliament list in this petition?

b Explain why parliament felt that the king's recent actions were actually illegal?

c What do you understand by (i) 'privy council' (line 13) (ii) 'writs of *Habeas Corpus*' (line 20) (iii) 'martial law' (line 38).

* d What tax *had* Charles I been levying before 1628 'without common consent by act of parliament' (lines 30 and 31)?

* e When and why had 'great companies of soldiers and mariners' been dispersed into several areas of the country (line 23)?

5 Ship Money 1636

The Lord-Keeper February 14 in the Star-Chamber spake to the Judges before they went their circuits to this effect . . . . He said, this was the third year his Majesty had issued Writs, requiring aid of his subjects for the guard of the dominion of the Seas and safety of the Kingdom. In the
5 first year, when they were directed to the ports and maritime places only, there was little opposition; but when in the second year they went generally throughout the Kingdom, they were disobeyed by some, in maritime as well as inland countries, and actions have been brought against persons imployed about the execution of those writs. He said,
10 none could expect that *Arcana Regis* [Secrets of the King] should be made publick, but such reasons as are fit to be opened are these: 1. Our safety is concerned, for if we lose the dominion of the seas, we lie open to all dangers. 2. We are concerned in point of honour, that we keep that dominion. 3. In point of profit to preserve our trade, which inriches the
15 inland as well as maritime places, by the vent of our wool, lead and other staple commodities . . . And when his Majesty understood some refused to pay, he writ his letter to them, the Judges, for their opinions, who returned him an answer under their own hands.

. . . The Judges opinions were in these following words, *viz.* That
20 when the good and safety of the Kingdom in general is concerned, and the Kingdom in danger, your Majesty may by writ under the Great Seal of England, command all your subjects of this your Kingdom, at their charge to provide and furnish such a number of ships, with men, victuals

25 and ammunition, and for such time as your Majesty shall think fit, for the defence and safeguard of this Kingdom from such danger and peril; and that by law your Majesty may compel the doing thereof, in case of refusal; and that in such case, your Majesty is the sole judge of the danger, and when and how the same is to be prevented and avoided.

J. Rushworth, *Historical Collections*, 1659, Vol II, pp 262–3

Questions

a What justification is given for the extension of Ship Money to inland as well as maritime counties?

b Explain why the king had (i) informed the judges of the background to Ship Money before they visited their circuits (ii) obtained the opinion of the judges concerning his right to charge the tax.

c Explain what you understand by (i) 'the Star-Chamber' (line 1) (ii) 'by writ under the Great Seal of England' (lines 21–22).

* d Give examples of 'some [who] refused to pay' (lines 16 and 17).

* e In view of the justification given here for the tax, why did members of the Short Parliament speak so bitterly against it? (See also document 7 in this section.)

6   Grievances against Charles I

. . . Some other parliaments there were, but still abruptly broken up when they put forward any endeavour to redress grievances. The protestants abroad were all looked upon as puritans, and their interests, instead of being protected, sadly betrayed; ships were let out to the French
5 King to serve against them; and all the flower of the English gentry were lost in an ill-managed expedition to the Isle of Rhee, under pretence of helping them, but so ordered that it proved the loss of Rochelle, the strong fort and best defence of all the protestants in France. Those in Germany were no less neglected in all treaties, although his own sister and
10 her children were so highly concerned. The whole people were sadly grieved at these misgovernments, and, loath to impute them to the King, cast all the odium upon the Duke of Buckingham, whom at length a discontented person stabbed, believing he did God and his country good service by it. All the Kingdom, except the duke's own dependents and
15 kindred, rejoiced in the death of this duke; but they found little cause, for after it the King still persisted in his design of enslaving them, and found other ministers ready to serve his self-willed ambition, such as were Noy, his attorney-general, who set on foot that hateful tax of ship-money, and many more illegal exactions . . . . Besides these, and a great rascally
20 company of flatterers and projectors, there were all the corrupted, tottering bishops . . . . But there were two above all the rest, who led the van of the King's evil counsellors, and these were Laud, archbishop of Canterbury, a fellow of mean extraction and arrogant pride, and the Earl

of Strafford, who as much outstripped all the rest in favour as he did in
abilities, being a man of deep policy, stern resolution, and ambitious zeal
to keep up the glory of his own greatness . . . . But above all these the
King had another instigator of his own violent purpose, more powerful
than all the rest, and that was the queen, who, grown out of her
childhood, began to turn her mind . . . to that which did less become
her, and was more fatal to the Kingdom; which is never in any place
happy where the hands which were made only for distaffs affect the
management of sceptres.

> Lucy Hutchinson, *Memoirs of the Life of Colonel Hutchinson*, 1846,
> pp 86—9

Questions

a Which particular grievances against the government of Charles I are
listed here?

b What reasons are given for these mistaken policies?

c Analyse this passage carefully, separating those words and phrases
which are based on historical fact from those which stem from the
writer's personal feelings and bias.

* *d* Explain details of (i) the 'ill-managed expedition to the Isle of Rhee'
(line 6) (ii) 'that hateful tax of ship-money' (line 18).

* *e* Who were (i) 'his . . . sister' (line 9) (ii) 'a discontented person' (line
13) (iii) 'the queen' (line 28).

* *f* What particular policies do you link with (i) Archbishop Laud (line
22) (ii) the Earl of Strafford (lines 23 and 24).

7   The Short Parliament 1640

The Parliament met according to summons upon the 13th of April in the
year 1640, with the usual ceremony and formality; and, after the King
had shortly mentioned his desire to be again acquainted with Parliaments
after so long an intermission, and to receive the advice and assistance of his
subjects there, he referred the cause of their present convention to be
enlarged upon by the Lord Keeper; who related the whole proceedings of
Scotland . . . who told them, after the whole relation, that his majesty
did not expect advice from them . . . but that they should, as soon as
might be, give his majesty such a supply as he might provide for the
vindication of his honour by raising an army; . . . and his majesty assured
them, if they would gratify him with this expedition, that he would give
them time enough afterwards to represent any grievances to him, and a
favourable answer to them . . . .

Whilst men gazed upon each other, looking who should begin (much
the greatest part having never before sat in Parliament), Mr. Pimm, a man
of good reputation, but much better known afterward, who had been as
long in those assemblies as any man then living, brake the ice; and, in a set

discourse of above two hours, after mention of the King with the most profound reverence and commendation of his wisdom and justice, he
20 observed that by the long intermission of Parliaments many unwarrantable things had been practised . . . . Mr. Grimston insisted only on the business of ship-money . . . . Peard, a bold lawyer, of little note, inveighed more passionately against it, calling it 'an abomination' . . . .

After some days had been passed in this manner, and it not being in
25 view when this debate would be at an end, the King sent a message in writing to the Commons by Sir Harry Vane, who was now both Secretary of State and Treasurer of the Household, and at that time of good credit there; wherein his majesty . . . made this proposition, that, if the Parliament would grant him twelve subsidies, to be paid in three
30 years . . . his majesty would then release all his title or pretence to ship-money for the future . . . . Both Sir H. Vane and the Solicitor General Harbert had made a worse representation of the humour and affection of the House than it deserved, and undertook to know that if they came together again they would pass such a vote against ship-money as would
35 blast that revenue and other branches of the receipt . . . . They two, and they only, wrought so far with the King that, without so much deliberation as the affair was worthy of, his majesty the next morning, which was on the fourth or fifth of May, not three weeks from their first meeting, sent for the Speaker to attend him and . . . dissolved the
40 Parliament.

Clarendon, *History of the Rebellion*, Vol 1, pp 173–83

Questions

a What request and what promise did Charles make at the assembling of this parliament?

b What proved to be the greatest stumbling-block to the speedy granting of the king's request? How did Charles attempt to overcome this problem?

c How far, according to Clarendon, was the king to blame for the untimely dissolution of this parliament?

* d Explain what is meant by 'the whole proceedings of Scotland' (lines 6 and 7).

* e What do we learn about Pym from this extract? Why did he become 'much better known afterward' (line 16)?

* f What is there here to suggest that Vane later changed his allegiance? Mention any important action taken by him subsequently.

8 Charles I and the Five Members 1642

. . . As soon as the House met again, 'twas moved, considering there was an intention to take these five men away by force, to avoid all tumult, let them be commanded to absent themselves . . . . A little after, the King

came, with all his guard, and all his pensioners, and two or three hundred
soldiers and gentlemen. The King commanded the soldiers to stay in the
hall, and sent us word he was at the door. The Speaker was commanded
to sit still, with the mace lying before him, and then the King came to the
door . . . and commanded all that came with him, upon their lives not to
come in. So the doors were kept open, and the Earl of Roxburgh stood
within the door, leaning upon it. Then the King came upwards, towards
the chair, with his hat off, and the Speaker stepped out to meet him. Then
the King stepped up to his place, and stood upon the Step, but sat not
down in the chair. And, after he had looked a great while, he told us, he
would not break our privileges, but treason had no privilege; he came for
those five gentlemen, for he expected obedience yesterday, and not an
answer. Then he called Mr. Pym, and Mr. Holles, by name, but no
answer was made. Then he asked the Speaker if they were here, or where
they were. Upon that the Speaker fell on his knees and desired his excuse,
for he was a servant to the House, and had neither eyes, nor tongue, to see
or say anything but what they commanded him. Then the King told him,
he thought his own eyes were as good as his, and then said, his birds were
flown, but he did expect the House would send them to him, and if they
did not he would seek them himself, for their treason was foul and such an
one as they would all thank him to discover. Then he assured us they
should have a fair trial, and so went out, putting off his hat till he came to
the door.

Memoirs of the Verney Family during the Civil War, Vol 1, p 36

Questions

a In what ways did the king in this episode endeavour to show some
respect for (i) the House of Commons (ii) the law of the land?

b What indication is there to suggest that the Speaker was now much
more in sympathy with the House than he had been in 1628? (See also
document 3 in this section.)

* *c* Who were the Five Members? Why did the king accuse them of
treason?

* *d* Which 'privileges' had, in the view of the Commons, been broken by
the king as a result of this incident?

II Laud and the Puritans
1628—41

Introduction

The passionate attempt made by Puritans during the 1570s to overthrow both Prayer Book and bishops had, by the arrival of the Stuarts, largely abated. Radical reform seemed far less urgent once the threat posed by the forces of the Counter-Reformation had been averted. Mary, queen of Scots was dead. The Spanish Armada had been defeated. During the first years of James I's reign, therefore, Puritans were generally content to discuss possible modifications to the existing church and improvement in the quality of clergy. This comparative calm, was, however, shattered by the outbreak of the Thirty Years War in 1618. Protestantism was again under attack. Gradually, but with growing vigour, Puritans again voiced their demands in parliament, in the pulpit and in the press for basic reform of the Prayer Book and church government. This alone, they believed, could strengthen them to face the catholic assault.

Any possibility of a compromise between the Puritans and the anglican church was completely shattered by the appointment of William Laud as bishop of London in 1628. By 1633, when he became archbishop of Canterbury, Laud's friends and followers occupied nearly all the other bishoprics in the country. Together they shared his belief that bishops were appointed by divine right, thus emphasising the authority they claimed in church government. Together they pursued his policy which aimed at bringing order back into the church, 'the upholding of the external worship of God in it, and the settling of it to the rules of its first reformation'. This meant placing a greater stress on the sacraments, re-siting and railing off the altar in the chancel, restoring vestments and ceremony. It meant resisting any interference from laity (whether churchwardens or justices) in clerical matters. It meant placing restrictions on the activities of travelling 'lecturers'.

Fearful that catholicism was beginning to show itself, parliament voiced puritan feeling in its repeated attacks on these innovations. Its criticisms, however, were totally silenced during Charles I's Personal Rule between 1629 and 1640. Laud was free to develop his ideas unhindered – with support, where necessary, from the Courts of High Commission and Star Chamber. But he overplayed his hand. An attempt to impose a new Prayer Book on the Scots in 1637 ended in war. The inevitable recall of the English parliament in 1640 unleashed a storm of anger against Laud and his unpopular policies. Before the year was out, the archbishop was in prison on a charge of high treason.

Further Reading

William M. Lamont, *Marginal Prynne* (Routledge, 1963)
William M. Lamont, *Godly Rule* (Macmillan, 1969)
H. R. Trevor-Roper, *Archbishop Laud* (Macmillan, 1940)

1 Puritans and the Sabbath 1615

We lived in a country that had but little preaching at all. In the village where I was born there were four readers successively in six years' time, ignorant men and two of them immoral in their lives, who were all my schoolmasters. In the village where my father lived, there was a reader of
5 about eighty years of age that never preached and had two churches about twenty miles distant; his eyesight failing him he said Common prayer without book, but for the reading of the psalms and chapters he got a common thresher and day labourer one year, and a tailor another year . . . .
10   In the village where I lived the reader read the Common prayer briefly, and the rest of the day even till dark night almost, excepting eating time, was spent in dancing under a maypole and a great tree, not far from my father's door, where all the town did meet together. And though one of my father's own tenants was the piper, he could not restrain him nor
15 break the sport, so that we could not read the Scriptures in our family without the great disturbance of the tabor and pipe and noise in the street. Many times my mind was inclined to be among them and sometimes I broke loose from conscience and joined with them, and the more I did it the more I was inclined to it. But when I heard them call my father
20 Puritan, it did much to cure me and alienate me from them, for I considered my father's exercise of reading the Scriptures was better than theirs and would surely be better thought on by all men at the last. . . . For my Father never scrupled Common prayer or Ceremonies, nor spake against Bishops, nor ever so much as prayed but by a book or
25 form, being not ever acquainted then with any that did otherwise. But only for reading Scriptures when the rest were dancing on the Lord's Day, and for praying (by a form out of the end of the Common prayer Book) in his house, and for reproving drunkards and swearers, and for talking sometimes a few words of Scripture and the Life to come, he was
30 reviled commonly by the name of Puritan and Hypocrite, and so were the godly conformable ministers that lived anywhere in the country near us, not only by our neighbours, but by the common talk of the vulgar

rabble of all about us. By this experience I was fully convinced that Godly
People were the best, those that despised them and lived in sin and
35 pleasure were a malignant unhappy sort of people; and this kept me out of
their Company, except now and then when the love of sports and play
enticed me.

Richard Baxter, *Reliquiae Baxterianae* 1696, pp 1–3

Questions

a What were the main hindrances in Baxter's village to the spread of
   Christianity?
b Why did his father object to the dancing?
c Explain why his father seems to have been less extreme than many
   Puritans of the time.
* d How did local disagreements over maypole dancing eventually lead
      to a clash between the Puritans and Archbishop Laud (with the king's
      support)?

2 The Declaration of Sports 1618 and 1633

The Lord Chief Justice Richardson and Baron Denham, at the Assizes for
the County of Somerset . . . again ordered, That Revels, Church Ales,
Clerk Ales and all other publick Ales should be utterly
suppressed. . . . But the Archbishop of Canterbury hearing of this
5 Proceeding of the Judges in Church affairs, and imposing upon the
Ministers to publish their Order without the consent of the Bishop of the
Diocese, complained thereof to the King; and the Chief Justice being
summoned to attend the Council, alleged for himself that the Order was
made at the request of all the Justices of Peace upon the Bench, and upon
10 view of divers antient Precedents; Nevertheless he was commanded to
revoke his Order. . . . The Justices of the Peace were troubled at this
Revocation, and drew up a Petition to the King subscribed by the Lord
Pawlet, Sir John Stawell, Sir Ralph Hopton, Sir Francis Docklington
etc. . . . but the delivery thereof was prevented by the coming forth of
15 the King's Declaration concerning lawful Sports on the Lord's day after
Evening Prayer, dated 18 Octob. which was to this effect.

That King James in his return from Scotland, coming thro Lancashire,
and finding his subjects debarred from lawful Recreations upon Sunday,
after Evening Prayer and upon Holidays; and considering that by this
20 means the meaner sort, who labour hard all the week, should have no
recreations at all: And after his Return, seeing his Subjects in other parts
suffer in the same kind, did in the year 1618, publish a Declaration of this
Tenor, *viz.* Whereas the last year, upon his return from
Scotland . . . with his own Ears he heard the general complaint of the
25 People, that they were barred from all lawful Recreations upon the
Sundays, after the ending of all Divine Service, which produces two

Feuds: 1. It hinders the Conversion of many, whom their Priests persuade, that no honest Mirth or Recreation is lawful in the Religion the King professeth. 2. This Prohibition barreth the common people from
30 using such Exercises as may make their Bodies more able for war, and instead thereof sets up Tipling and Drunkenness, and breeds discontented Speeches; for when can the common People have Recreation, if not upon Sundays and Holidays? His Majesty's Pleasure therefore is . . . that after Divine Service his People be not disturbed or discouraged from any
35 lawful Recreation, as Dancing either Men or Women, Archery for Men, Leaping, Vaulting, having of May-games, Whitson Ales, Morrice Dances and Maypoles, so as it be without impediment or neglect of Divine Service; and Women may carry Rushes for decorating the Church as formerly; but Bear and Bull-baiting, and Interludes on
40 Sunday, and Bowling at all times in the meaner sort was prohibited; and known recusants, and those that are not present at Church before their going to the said Recreations, were debarred this Liberty, and such as use those Exercises before the end of all Divine Service were to be punished . . . .
45 Now his present Majesty (K. Charles) doth ratify and publish this his Blessed Father's Declaration, the rather, for that there hath been of late in some counties a general Forbidding, not only of ordinary Meetings, but of the Feasts of the Dedication of Churches, commonly called Wakes, which his Pleasure is, shall with others be observed; . . . he commands all
50 his Judges, Justices of the Peace, Mayors etc. to take notice hereof, and that Publication hereof be made by order from the Bishops thro all Parish Churches. But this Declaration proved a snare to many Ministers, otherwise very conformable, several who refused to read the same in the Church being suspended or silenced.

J. Rushworth, *Historical Collections*, 1659 Vol II, pp 166–9

Questions

a Why did Archbishop Laud object to the action of the Lord Chief Justices in Somerset?

b Why were the Justices 'troubled at this Revocation' of the order (lines 11 and 12)?

* c From the evidence in this and the preceding extract, what *types* of people were (i) for (ii) against sport on Sundays?

d What four main arguments had James I used to support Sunday sport?

* e Explain what you understand by (i) Church Ales (line 2) (ii) Wakes (line 48), (iii) the Council (line 8), (iv) recusants (line 41), (v) conformable (line 53).

* f Write on the later importance of Sir Ralph Hopton (line 13).

3   Archbishop Laud's 'Innovations'

This year (1634) being the first of Bishop Laud's translation to
Canterbury, great offence was taken at his setting up pictures in the
windows of his Chappels at Lambeth and Croydon, the portraiture being
made according to the Roman Missal, his bowing towards the Table or
5   Altar, and using Copes at the Sacrament, which the people clamoured
against as popish, superstitious and idolatrous . . . .

Mr. Samuel Ward, a minister in Ipswich, preached against the
common bowing at the name of Jesus, and against the King's Book of
Sports, and said that the Church of England was ready to ring changes in
10   religion, and the Gospel stood on tiptoe as ready to be gone; for this he
was suspended in the High Commission (1635) and enjoined recantation,
which he refusing, was committed to prison, where he lay a long
time . . . .

Mr. Chancey, Minister of Ware in Hartfordshire, for opposing the
15   making of a rail about the communion-table in that parish Church was
brought into the High Commission (1635) and suspended from his
ministry till he made in open court a recantation after a prescribed form,
acknowledging his offence and protesting he was persuaded that kneeling
at the sacrament was a lawful and commendable gesture; and that the rail
20   set up in the cancel with a bench thereunto annexed for kneeling at the
communion, was a decent and convenient ornament, and promising
conformity in all things. He was condemned in great costs of suit and
imprisoned. Afterwards he made his recantation and was dismissed with
an admonition from the Archbishop.
25   J. Rushworth, *Historical Collections*, 1659, Vol II, pp 219, 239,
247–8

The 19th of December (1638) I came acquainted with Mr. Tim
Thurscross a Prebend of York . . . . He is a man of late greatly mortified,
having within less than this half year resigned unto the Archbishop of
30   York his Archdeaconrie and Vicaridge of Kerby Moorside, being much
troubled in his conscience for having obtained them thro symonie, and
now living at York hath nothing to maintain himself and his wife withall
but his Prebend. He preacheth every Sunday at one place or other, and his
wife betakes herself to get her living by teaching young children to sow.
35   He is a man of most holy life, only he is conformable to the church
discipline that now is used and to those late imposed ceremonies of
bowing and adoring towards the altar.

When I asked him his opinion concerning that, I thought it came too
near idolatry to adore a place with rich cloaths and other furniture and to
40   command to use towards it bodily worship: to which he answered that his
bowing was not to the altar but to God especially in that
place . . . . This man bestowed a great part of the day in prayer with
much fasting, he riseth at 4 o'clock in the morning and is at prayer in

private and with his family until six, at which time he goes to the Minster
45 prayers . . . .
Rev. D. Parsons (ed.), The Diary of Sir Henry Slingsby, pp 7–9

That the Lords the Bishops . . . take great care concerning the lecturers
within their several dioceses, for whom we give them special directions
following:
50 1. That in all parishes the afternoon sermons be turned into catechising
by questions and answers, where and whence ever there is not some great
cause apparent to break this ancient and profitable order.
2. That every Bishop take care in his diocese that all the lecturers do read
Divine Service according to the liturgy printed by authority, in their
55 surplices and hoods, before the lecture.
3. That where a lecture is set up in a market town it may be read by a
company of grave and orthodox near adjoining and of the same diocese,
and that they ever preach in such seemly habits as belong to their degrees,
and not in cloaks.
60 4. That if a corporation maintains a single lecturer he be not suffered to
preach till he professes his willingness to take upon him a living with cure
of souls within that corporation, and that he do actually take such benefice
or cure so soon as it shall be fairly procured for him.
Laud's Instructions to Bishops, 1633

Questions

a Explain the controversy over altars, mentioning the significance of
(i) the rail (lines 15 and 19) (ii) their positioning in the chancel (line
20) (iii) the bench for kneeling (line 20) (iv) bowing (line 4) (v) the
terms 'table' and 'altar' (lines 4 and 5).

b What other 'innovations' were regarded by some as being Roman
Catholic in origin?

* c What do you understand by 'the High Commission' (lines 11 and 16)?
Explain its importance during the 1630s.

d What do you understand by the terms (i) recantation (lines 12 and
17) (ii) 'symonie' (line 31) (iii) liturgy (line 54) (iv) cure of souls
(lines 61 and 62)?

* e Explain the controversy over lecturers. In what ways did Laud try to
restrict their activities in 1633?

4   The case of Prynne, Bastwick and Burton 1637

An Information was exhibited in the Starchamber by the Attorney
General against John Bastwick Doctor in Physick, Henry Burton
Batchelor of Divinity and William Pryn Barrister at Law defendants, for
writing and publishing seditious, schismatical and libellous books against
5 the Hierarchy . . . . Mr. Burton in his answer set forth the substance of

his sermon which he preached the fifth of November in his Parish Church in Friday-Street, touching the innovations brought into the Church. Dr. Bastwick in his answer termed the Prelates invaders of the King's Prerogative, contemners of the Scriptures, advancers of popery, super-
10 stition, idolatry, profaneness, oppression of the King's subjects, enemies of God and the King, and servants of the Devil. Mr. Pryn's answer was much against the Hierarchy, but in more moderate and cautious expressions.

June 14 The Lords being set in their places in the Star Chamber, and
15 the three defendants brought to the Bar to receive their sentences, the Lord Chief Justice Finch looking earnestly on Mr. Pryn said, It seemed to him that he had ears still notwithstanding his former censure: whereupon the Usher being commanded to turn up his hair, some of the Lords seemed displeased that his ears had not been cut closer off. But Mr. Pryn
20 answered, there was not one of them there but would have been sorry to have had his ears so cropped . . . .

The Court proceeded to sentence, fined the three defendants 5000 *l.* a-piece to the King, adjudged them all to stand in the pillory in the New Palace-yard in Westminster, Bastwick and Burton to lose their ears, and
25 Pryn the remainder of his ears; Pryn to be stigmatised on both cheeks with the letters S.L. signifying a seditious libeller: all of them to suffer perpetual imprisonment, Pyrn in Carnarvon Castle in Wales, Bastwick in Launceston Castle in Cornwell and Burton in Lancaster Castle . . . .

June 30 The said three prisoners were brought to the New Palace-
30 yard at Westminster to suffer according to their sentence . . . . Mr. Burton spake much while in the pillory to the people: the executioner cut off his ears deep and close in a cruel manner with much effusion of blood, an artery being cut, as there was likewise of Dr. Bastwick: then Mr. Pryn's cheeks were seared with an iron made exceeding hot, which done,
35 the executioner cut off one of his ears and a piece of his cheek with it; then hacking the other ear almost off, he left it hanging and went down; but being called up again, he cut it quite off.

The Starchamber having ordered the three prisoners to be conveyed to the said three remote castles, and that during their imprisonment they
40 should not be admitted to the use of pen, ink or paper, or of any book but the Bible, Common Prayer Book and other canonical books of devotion; they were conveyed thither accordingly: the wives of Bastwick and Burton being hardly permitted to speak with their husbands by the way. The chamber in Launceston Castle where Dr. Bastwick was lodged, was
45 so ruinous that every small blast of wind threatened to shatter it down upon his head; and the Lord Chief Justice Finch being informed thereof, said that the Doctor by his faith and prayer would hold it from falling.

J. Rushworth, *Historical Collections*, 1659, Vol II, pp 273, 283, 293-5

Questions

* *a* Explain the importance of the Court of Star Chamber (line 1) during the 1630s.
  b What, in your own words, were the main complaints against bishops expressed by Prynne, Bastwick and Burton?
* *c* Explain the significance of 'he had ears still notwithstanding his former censure' (line 17).
  d What do you understand by the term 'seditious libeller' (line 26)?
  e What indications suggest that the writer of this extract sympathised with the three accused?

5 Archbishop Laud's Defence of Bishops 1637

For my care of this Church, the reducing of it into order, the upholding of the external worship of God in it, and the settling of it to the rules of its first reformation, are the causes (and the sole causes, whatever are pretended) of all this malicious storm, which hath lowered so black upon
5 me, and some of my brethren. And in the meantime, they which are the only, or the chief innovators of the Christian world, having nothing to say, accuse us of innovation; they themselves and their complices in the meantime being the greatest innovators that the Christian world hath almost ever known . . . .
10 Our main crime is (would they all speak out, as some of them do), that we are bishops; were we not so, some of us might be as passable as other men. And a great trouble 'tis to them, that we maintain that our calling of bishops is *jure divino*, by divine right . . . . And I say further, that from the Apostles' times, in all ages, in all places, the Church of Christ was
15 governed by bishops; and lay-elders never heard of, till Calvin's new-fangled device at Geneva.
Now this is made by these men, as if it were *contra Regem*, against the King, in right or in power. But that's a mere ignorant shift; for our being bishops *jure divino*, by divine right, takes nothing from the King's right or
20 power over us. For though our office be from God and Christ immediately, yet may we not exercise that power, either of order or jurisdiction, but as God hath appointed us, that is, not in his Majesty's or any Christian King's kingdoms, but by and under the power of the King given us so to do . . . .
25 Next, supposing our calling, as bishops, could not be made good *jure divino*, by divine right, yet *jure ecclesiastico*, by ecclesiastical right, it cannot be denied. And here in England the bishops are confirmed, both in their power and means, by Act of Parliament . . . . Therefore, all these libels, so far forth as they are against our calling, are against the King and the
30 law, and can have no other purpose than to stir up sedition among the people . . . .
For the main scope of their libels is to kindle a jealousy in men's minds

that there are some great plots in hand, dangerous plots (so says Mr.
Burton expressly) to change the orthodox religion established in
35   England, and to bring in, I know not what, Romanish superstition in the
room of it. As if the external decent worship of God could not be upheld
in this Kingdom, without bringing in Popery.

Laud's Speech at the Trial of Prynne, Bastwick and Burton

Questions

* *a*   Explain how Laud, during the 1630s, had pursued a church policy of
'reducing . . . it into order' and 'upholding . . . the external worship of God' (lines 1 and 2).
  b   By what right, according to Laud, did bishops rule the church? Why
did this not conflict with the powers of king and parliament?
* *c*   What do you understand by (i) 'the rules of its first reformation' (lines
2 and 3) (ii) 'Calvin's new-fangled device at Geneva' (lines 15 and 16)? ·
  d   Why did Laud so resent the attacks made by Prynne, Bastwick and
Burton?

6   The New Scottish Prayer Book 1637

This Service-book was first appointed by Proclamation to be read in all
churches on Easter-day, 1637, but afterwards deferred till the 23rd of
July, and to be read only in the churches of Edinburgh and parts adjacent.
Accordingly it was then begun to be read in Edinburgh in St. Giles's
5   Church (commonly called the Great Church) many of the Council, both
the Archbishops, divers other Bishops, the Lords of the Session, the
Magistrates of Edinburgh and a great auditory being present. No sooner
had the Dean of Edinburgh opened the Book, but there were among the
meaner sort (especially the women) clapping of hands and hideous
10   execrations and outcries. The Bishop of Edinburgh (who was to preach)
went into the pulpit, thinking to appease the tumult, and presently a stool
was thrown at his head. The Provost and Bailiffs at length thrust out of
the Church those that made the tumult and shut the doors against them;
then the Dean read the service. But such were the outcries, rapping at the
15   doors and throwing in of stones at the windows, crying, *A Pape, a Pape,
Antichrist, pull him down*, that the Bailiffs were forced to come again to
appease their fury. Service and Sermon ended, the Bishop of Edinburgh
repairing home, was near trodden to death, but rescued by some who
observed his danger . . . .
20   That in the new Service-book which most startled the Scots, was the
omission at the delivery of the Bread in the sacrament of these words, *And
take and eat this, in remembrance that Christ died for thee, and feed on him in
thine heart by faith with thanksgiving*; and the omission at the delivery of the
wine of these words, *And drink this, in remembrance that Christ's blood was
25   shed for thee, and be thankful*; although these passages are both in the

English Liturgy, and do expressly take away all opinion of any Transubstantiation, or corporeal eating of Christ's Body, or drinking his Blood in the Sacrament; so that there was nothing left at the delivery of the Bread and Wine, but the preceding words in the English Liturgy, *The Body of our Lord Jesus Christ etc.* and, *The Blood of our Lord Jesus Christ etc.* which the aforesaid words expunged out of the Scotch Liturgy did qualify and explain. But thus standing alone in this new Liturgy, these are the very same words that are in the Roman Missal, without any other addition than *Amen*, to be pronounced by the receiver. What the meaning hereof was, appears not; but the Scots apprehended it the prologue to the bringing in among them a principal point of Popery, to wit, the Doctrine of Transubstantiation.

> J. Rushworth, *Historical Collections*, 1659, Vol II, pp 298–9, 304–5

Questions

a What methods were used to show opposition to the Prayer Book? Is there any evidence to indicate that this was organised in advance?

* *b* Explain fully the doctrine of transubstantiation (line 27). What did the Puritans believe in relation to this? Why was the Prayer Book wording so vital?

* *c* What main fear runs through this extract? In which other extracts in this section is the same fear expressed?

7 Laud's Bond with the Puritans

'Begin with an individual and before you know it you find that you have created a type; begin with a type, and you find that you have created – nothing.' When we discuss Archbishop Laud we begin with a type and usually end with nothing – nothing, that is, except clichés about the abasement of Church before Crown. The type was the creation of Lord Macaulay. Archbishop Laud, 'minuting down his dreams, counting the drops of blood which fall from his nose, watching the direction of the salt, and listening for the note of the screech-owl', becomes, in Macaulay's splendidly contemptuous prose, the type of the royal creature. He becomes a Sir Thomas More upside down: God's good servant, but the King's first. Most modern political historians have been influenced by Macaulay's brilliantly unfair judgement . . . .

Even Macaulay, the most eloquent advocate of the view of Laud as a royal lapdog, could not ignore passages in Laud's correspondence with Strafford that conveyed piety and a sense of duty to God. Macaulay entertained for Laud 'a more unmitigated contempt than for any other character in our history' . . . . He had no doubts, then, that this supposed piety merely cloaked self-interest . . . . The lie to Macaulay's sneer comes direct from Laud's diary . . . . The diary, however, repays close

20 attention as an extraordinary, moving record of one man's hopes and
fears. It is an authentic puritan document. And Puritan opponents, who
loathed Laud's innovations in church ceremonies, were curiously blind to
the bonds that united him with them. This led them into a serious blunder
in 1645. They seized his diary and published it in the hope of discrediting
25 him. Instead, Laud's Puritan opponents found themselves strangely
drawn to a man, possessed like them of a vision, assured of its rectitude,
but driven to record with painful honesty the temptations and backslid-
ings on the path to that goal. Almost against their will, William Walwyn
and Henry Robinson were impressed by the 'signes of a mortall noble
30 pious minde' in his diary, although they added an important rider:
'according to such weak principles as hee had been bred up in'. In other
words: they abhorred what he *stood* for, not what he *strove* for.
Conversely we shall see that after 1660 Laud's followers might restore
what he stood for, but they could not restore what he strove for.
35 Episcopacy was restored, but not the ideal of the Unity of Jerusalem nor
the instruments – the Court of Star Chamber, the Court of High
Commission, the clerical visitations – to implement that ideal. The
Restoration Church was not, except in superficial matters, Laudian.

William M. Lamont, *Godly Rule*, 1969, pp 56, 69–70

Questions

* *a* Explain what do you understand by (i) 'a Sir Thomas More upside
  down' (line 10) (ii) 'the Unity of Jerusalem' (line 35).
  b Why is Laud's diary described here as 'an authentic puritan document'
  (line 21)?
* *c* Who was Lord Macaulay? Why does Lamont feel that he was wrong
  in his judgement of Laud's character?
* *d* Why do you think that 'most modern political historians have been
  influenced by Macaulay's brilliantly unfair judgement' (lines 11 and
  12)? What causes such unfair judgements to be made in the first place?
  How do later historians sometimes manage to correct mistaken
  interpretations?

III The Gentry Controversy

Introduction

In 1941 Professor R. H. Tawney launched what was to become a fierce and often bitter debate on the origins of the English Civil War. His views were expounded in two articles – *Harrington's Interpretation of His Age* and *The Rise of the Gentry, 1558–1640*. He argued that the crisis which flared up ˙in the middle of the seventeenth century was largely the outcome of shifting economic and social fortunes. The long-established nobility were in decline, victims of their own extravagance and mounting inflation. The gentry were on the rise, opportunist in outlook and business-like in approach. Civil war enabled this latter group to modify the country's political structure, obtaining for themselves within it a place worthy of their new social and economic status. Further support to this theory was given in 1948 by Lawrence Stone who, in an article entitled *The Anatomy of the Elizabethan Aristocracy*, emphasised that the dramatic decline of the aristocracy had been caused by wasteful expenditure.

Battle was really joined however in 1951, when H. R. Trevor-Roper published an article (*The Elizabethan Aristocracy: an Anatomy Anatomised*) violently attacking Stone's interpretation of statistical evidence. Stone replied one year later with an amended version of his earlier thesis (*The Elizabethan Aristocracy: A Restatement*). Meanwhile Trevor-Roper was preparing another assault, this time on the views of Tawney himself. In an essay, *The Gentry 1540–1640*, published in 1953, he countered Tawney's ideas by advocating a new theory of his own. Whereas office-holders and other court favourites continued to rise, the 'mere' gentry (whose livelihood was based solely on land) suffered a steady decline in fortune. By 1640 these disgruntled gentry had formed the 'country' party which led the opposition against Charles I. They were eventually to be identified as the Independents who overthrew the monarchy. J. P. Cooper completed the undermining of Tawney and Stone by casting serious doubts on the validity of their statistical approach in an article entitled *The Counting of Manors* (1956).

A few years later, however, Trevor-Roper himself was under attack, first from Christopher Hill in *Recent Interpretations of the Civil War* (1958) and then from Perez Zagorin in *The Social Interpretations of the English Revolution* (1959). Together they criticised him for lack of statistical evidence and for invalid assumptions about profits from agriculture and identity of the Independents. Meanwhile, in 1958, J. H. Hexter had offered a new theory on the *military* decline of the aristocracy (*Storm over the Gentry*) which had created a power vacuum by 1640. Lawrence Stone ventured back into the arena in 1965 with a scholarly book, *The Crisis of the Aristocracy*, based on massive research. Here he argued that the aristocracy had suffered a decline in power and prestige which left the monarchy vulnerable to attack in the crisis of 1640.

The debate on the Gentry Controversy will doubtless continue. But it does raise certain questions which are worthy of discussion. What was the point of it all? Why did this particular debate arouse so much personal bitterness amongst historians? Why do interpretations of the period keep changing?

Further Reading

R. C. Richardson, *The Debate on the English Revolution* (Methuen, 1977)
Conrad Russell (ed.), *The Origins of the English Civil War* (Macmillan, 1973)
Lawrence Stone, *Social Change and Revolution in England, 1540–1640* (Longman, 1965)

1 Tawney: Rise of the Gentry – Economic Decline of the Aristocracy

Observers became conscious, in the later years of Elizabeth, of an alteration in the balance of social forces, and a stream of comment began which continued to swell, until, towards the close of the next century, a new equilibrium was seen to have been reached. Its theme was the
5 changing composition . . . of the upper strata of the social pyramid. It was, in particular . . . the increase in the wealth and influence of certain intermediate groups, compared with the nobility, the Crown and the mass of small land-holders. Of those groups the most important, 'situated', as one of its most brilliant members wrote, 'neither in the lower
10 grounds . . . nor in the highest mountains . . . but in the valleys between both', was the squirearchy and its connections . . . .

In spite, nevertheless, of ambiguities, the group concerned was not difficult to identify. Its members varied widely in wealth; but though ragged at its edges, it had a solid core. That core consisted of the landed
15 proprietors, above the yeomanry, and below the peerage, together with a growing body of well-to-do farmers, sometimes tenants of their relatives, who had succeeded the humble peasants of the past as lessees of demesne farms; professional men, also rapidly increasing in number, such as the more eminent lawyers, divines, and an occasional medical practitioner,
20 and the wealthier merchants, who, if not, as many were, themselves sons

of landed families, had received a similar education, moved in the same circles, and in England, unlike France, were commonly recognised to be socially indistinguishable from them. It was this upper layer of commoners, heterogeneous, but compact, whose rapid rise in wealth and power most impressed contemporaries . . . .

The facts were plain enough. The ruin of famous families by personal extravagance and political ineptitude; the decline in the position of the yeomanry towards the turn of the century, when long leases fell in; the loss, not only of revenue, but also of authority, by the monarchy, as Crown lands melted; the mounting fortunes of the residuary legatee, a gentry whose aggregate income was put even in 1600 at some three times that of peers, bishops, deans and chapters, and richer yeomen together, and who steadily gathered into their hands estates slipping from the grasp of peasant, nobility, Church and Crown alike — such movements and their consequences were visible to all . . . .

Such a (noble) family, inheriting great estates, often inherited trouble. Its standards of expenditure were those of one age, its income that of another . . . . The overheads of a noble landowner — a great establishment, and often more than one; troops of servants and retainers; stables fit for a regiment of cavalry; endless hospitality to neighbours and national notabilities; visits to court, at once ruinous and unavoidable — had always been enormous. Now, on the top of these traditional liabilities, came the demands of a new world of luxury and fashion . . . . The wealth of some of the nobility, and especially of the older families, was not infrequently more spectacular than substantial. It was locked up in frozen assets . . . . Side by side with more lucrative possessions, their properties included majestic, but unremunerative franchises — hundreds, boroughs, fairs and markets; a multitude of Knights' fees, all honour and no profit; freeholds created in an age when falling, not rising, prices had been the great landowners' problem, and fixed rents were an insurance; hundreds of prickly copyholds whose occupants pocketed an unearned increment while the real income of their landlord fell . . . .

But to say that many noble families — though not they alone — encountered, in the two generations before the Civil War, a financial crisis is probably not an overstatement. The fate of the conservative aristocrat was, in fact, an unhappy one. Reduced to living 'like a rich beggar, in perpetual want', he sees his influence, popularity and property all melt together . . . . For, if the new world had its victims, it also had its conquerors. The conditions which depressed some incomes inflated others; and, while one group of landowners bumped heavily along the bottom, another, which was quicker to catch the tide when it turned, was floated to fortune . . . .

Under the pressure of an environment in motion, several types emerge. There is the gentleman farmer, leasing land, till he makes money, without owning it, and not infrequently — since the thing is his profession — running several farms at once. There is the man who works his land as a commercial undertaking — a John Toke in Kent, buying

Welsh and Scottish runts to finish on Romney Marsh for the London market; a Robert Loder in Berkshire, all piety and profits; a Sir Thomas Tresham in Northamptonshire, selling everything, from rabbits supplied on contract to a poulterer in Gracechurch Street, to wool to the value of £1,000 a year . . .; a Sir John Wynn in North Wales, cattle breeder, tribal chieftain, land-grabber, scholar, and prospector for minerals unknown to science . . . . There are families like the Pelhams and Twysdens, living mainly on rents, but doing on the side a useful trade in grain, hops, wool and iron in local markets and in London. Each type had its own idiosyncrasies, but none is in land for its health. All watch markets closely; buy and sell in bulk; compare the costs and yields of different crops; charge the rent, when custom allows, which a farm will stand; keep careful accounts. Mr. Fussell's description of one of them − 'before all things a business man' − is true of all. It was agricultural capitalists of this type who were making the pace, and to whom the future belonged.

R. H. Tawney, 'The Rise of the Gentry, 1558−1640', *Economic History Review*, XI (1941) pp 2, 4−5, 8−10, 12−13, 16−17

Questions

a   Who were the gentry? Explain why and how they had 'floated to fortune' (line 62).

b   What, according to Tawney, were the main causes of the decline of the aristocracy?

* c   Explain the meaning of 'copyholds' (line 51). Why were they 'prickly' in the seventeenth century? In what way did their occupants pocket 'an unearned increment' (line 51)?

* d   What were 'Knights' fees'? Why were they 'all honour and no profit' in the seventeenth century (line 48)? (See also extract 4).

* e   What consequences did inflation have for (i) the aristocracy (ii) the gentry? What were the main causes of this inflation during the period 1540−1640?

2   Trevor-Roper: Rise of the Office-Holders − Decline of the Mere Gentry

I believe that Professor Tawney's interpretation is evidentially weak . . . . The distinction between 'aristocracy' and 'gentry' is so entirely arbitrary that no useful conclusions can be based upon it . . . . While his aristocracy consists of a diminishing group of those families who happened to be noble at the beginning and still noble at the end of the period, his gentry consists both of the gentry who remained gentry throughout the period, and of those men who began as gentry and ended as peers, and of those who began as merchants, yeomen or anything else, and ended as gentry. No wonder the gentry, thus calculated, appear to 'rise' at the expense of the peerage . . . .

Is the evidence of economic difficulty (which may or may not be evidence of economic decline) inseparable from the nobility, and is the evidence of economic advance inseparable from the gentry? In my opinion the answer is clearly, No . . . . Peers and gentry had, on their different levels, the same problems, the same ambitions, the same conventions, the same tastes. Both were landlords; both had large families; both accepted the rule of primogeniture and the custom of entail; both had to find portions for daughters and younger sons. They built — according to their capacity — similar houses; they were buried in similar tombs . . . . The history of the Elizabethan and Jacobean gentry is strewn with their casualties, although Professor Tawney's searchlight, seeking to illuminate only prosperity among the gentry and aristocratic decline, has seldom lit upon them. If it has, he dismisses them as 'exceptions'. In this essay I shall hope to shed upon them a less flickering light . . . . I thus conclude that Professor Tawney's theory of the rise of the gentry at the expense of a declining peerage is a mistaken formulation . . . .

But there nevertheless is a phenomenon, which may still be called 'the rise of the gentry', and this phenomenon, even if it needs to be differently stated, still needs to be explained. The rising class may not have been 'the gentry' as distinct from 'the peerage'; but certain families within the landlord class — whether peers or gentry — undoubtedly did prosper and acquired, through their political machine the Houses of Parliament, a political power at the expense of the Crown. The question is, who were these families, and to what did they owe their prosperity?. . . Almost without exception they were office-holders. Cecils and Howards, Herberts and Villiers and their numerous kindred . . . .

Thus in an analysis of the 'new' peerage I find no adequate support for Professor Tawney's theory. Rather I conclude that whereas many families indubitably increased the yield of their lands, the great new fortunes were almost invariably made either by offices or in trade. Indeed, I would go further and say that between 1540 and 1640 land alone, without the help of offices or trade, even if it were improved, was hardly capable of causing the significant rise of any but a most exceptional family. For against the increased rents shown on estate accounts in this period must be placed the decline in the value of money . . . .

I have already suggested that office rather than land was the basis of many undoubtedly 'rising' families. I would now go further. Instead of the distinction between 'old' and 'new' landlords, between peers and gentry, I would suggest as the significant distinction of Tudor and Stuart landed society, the distinction between 'court' and 'country', between office-holders and the mere landlords. And by the words 'court' and 'office' I do not mean only the immediate members of the royal circle or the holders of political office: I use the words in the widest sense to cover all offices of profit under the crown — offices in the household, the administration and, above all — for it was most lucrative of all — the law; local office as well as central office, county lawyers as well as London lawyers, deputy-sheriffs as well as ministers, 'an auditor or vice-admiral

in his county' as well as a Teller of the Exchequer or a Warden of the Cinque Ports. These were the sheet anchors on which precarious
60 landlords depended in a storm . . . .

But what of the mere gentry who had no such positions? . . . . Perhaps, weary of the struggle, they would contract out of it altogether, spurn the Court and its offices . . . . Withdrawing from the Court, these men withdrew also from the ideology of the Court.
65 Some of them withdrew entirely and finally, into recusancy, from which – except through reconversion – there was no way back into public life; it was in the manor houses of the disgruntled country gentry that the missionary priests of the 1580s and 1590s found their converts and their secret refuges. Others withdrew less absolutely, into an opposite
70 ideology, the ideology of puritanism, and organised their opposition more hopefully in other country houses . . . .

The Great Rebellion is the central event of the seventeenth century in England, and any interpretation of English society which leaves unexplained that great convulsion is obviously unsatisfying. Now Professor
75 Tawney's thesis, in my opinion, leaves it unexplained, or rather, his explanation explains only his own thesis, not the facts. For what is his explanation? According to him, the Great Rebellion was the logical, though violent, culmination of the process which he imagines, a form of emphatic foreclosure by the creditor class of rising 'entrepreneur' gentry,
80 City merchants and lawyers, upon the mortgaged estates of a half-bankrupt peerage, Church and Crown: 'It was discovered, not for the last time, that as a method of foreclosure war was cheaper than litigation.'

But this explanation, while consistent with his theory, seems to me quite inadequate when we come to examine more closely the actual
85 course of the rebellion. For apart from the fact that the English peerage, on the eve of the Rebellion, was at least as rich as at any time in the preceding century, this explanation entirely leaves out of account the men who, more than any other, made the Great Rebellion – the men whose radicalism converted it from a series of political manoeuvres into
90 civil war and social revolution: the Independents . . . . They were not 'rising' gentry; they were not a creditor class; nor were they a sudden phenomenon of the 1640s. An examination of their claims, which were loud, and of their previous history, which is long seems to me to show that the Independents, the men whose spectacular actions have given a
95 revolutionary quality to a whole century, represent a class which Professor Tawney, in his interpretation of that period, has somehow overlooked, or at least has dismissed as insignificant temporary exceptions: the declining gentry . . . .

The decline in the mere gentry was not reversed by the accession of
100 King James; it was aggravated. For King James was interested in the Court, not the country. Extravagant where Elizabeth had been parsimonious, he was prepared to enrich his courtiers – at the cost of the country . . . . At the beginning of the reign of James I the gentry had been powerless against the apparently solid alliance of Crown, Court and

City; later in the same reign that alliance had begun to crumble, as
internal factions split the Court and the projects of alderman Cokayne
dismayed the City. Thus, the dissident gentry saw some of their old allies
returning to lead them and to exploit their grievances. Besides, unlike the
recusant gentry, the puritan gentry had an institution for the capture of
power. They had Parliament, if only they knew how to use it. From 1621
to 1629 a succession of uncontrollable Parliaments warned the Court of its
danger. Thereafter, for eleven years, there were no Parliaments. But it
was only the voice, not the hand, of opposition that was thus stilled.
Silently, in country-houses and caucus-meetings, the new course of
"Thorough" gradually cemented together a far more formidable
opposition . . . . In 1640, with discontented peers to lead them and City
money behind them, the gentry were again prepared to challenge the
court, and this time the court, incompetent and divided, was unprepared
for the struggle.

> H. R. Trevor-Roper, 'The Gentry 1540– 1640', *Economic History*
> *Review*, Supplement 1 (1953) pp 1, 4– 13, 26, 30– 5, 41– 2

Questions

* *a* Explain the terms (i) 'yeomen' (line 8) (ii) primogeniture' (line 17)
  (iii) 'entail' (line 17) (iv) 'the household' (line 54) (v) 'recusancy'
  (line 65).
  b What main criticisms does Trevor-Roper make of Tawney's *methods*
  as a historian?
  c What, according to Trevor-Roper, was the secret of success for those
  landowners who *did* prosper between 1540 and 1640?
  d What is meant by 'the mere gentry' (line 61)?
  e Explain how Trevor-Roper's explanation of the coming of the Civil
  War differs from that of Tawney.
* *f* From your knowledge of the period explain and comment on (i) 'For
  King James was interested in the Court, not the country' (lines 100
  and 101) (ii) 'the new course of "Thorough" gradually cemented
  together a far more formidable opposition' (lines 115 and 116).

3 Hill: Independence – not Declining Gentry

Although he criticises Professor Tawney's use of the category 'gentry',
Professor Trevor-Roper's own use of it is not altogether
satisfactory . . . . He seems to me to slide too easily from the concept of
'the mere gentry', 'the lesser gentry', to 'the declining gentry'. But the
lesser gentry included those who had successfully risen from the
yeomanry . . . . Indeed, Professor Trevor-Roper's use of his analysis to
explain the civil war is altogether unconvincing . . . . (He) has produced
no statistics at all. The declining gentry may or may not exist, may or may
not be politically significant, may or may not be Independents: but none

10 of this has been established statistically . . . .

Fortunately Mrs Keeler's recently-published biographical dictionary of *The Long Parliament* enables us to examine the Independent M.P.s in some detail. Over sixty of the M.P.s who sat after Pride's Purge were gentlemen whom it would be difficult to call either lesser or declining. At
15 least nine were lawyers, and as many had been courtiers or royal officials; many more came of lawyers' or courtiers' families. A number of those Independents who were 'mere' gentlemen entered the House as 're-cruiters' in 1645, and so cannot be used as evidence for the origins of the civil war. Wales and the western counties, which one would have
20 expected to contain a large proportion of 'mere' gentry, had a considerably *smaller* proportion of M.P.s in the Rump than did the rest of the country. When we look at the leaders of the Independents we encounter men of considerable wealth − Vane, Hesilrige, Mildmay, Pennington, Whitelocke. Henry Marten at first sight would seem to fit
25 Professor Trevor-Roper's conception of a declining gentleman who was an Independent, for all that most of us know of Marten is that he was a republican and heavily in debt. Closer investigation, however, reveals that he was the exact opposite of Professor Trevor-Roper's declining gentleman who used the civil war to recoup his fortunes; he was rich
30 enough to be a county M.P. in 1640, and incurred his debts by voluntary expenditure on Parliament's behalf during the civil war. Professor Trevor-Roper frequently mentions Oliver Cromwell as an Independent who was also a declining gentleman, and he is a more plausible example than most. But Cromwell would do equally well if one wished to prove
35 that the civil war was fought exclusively over religious issues. The really declining branch of the Cromwell family was that of the extravagant Sir Oliver de Hinchingbrooke − the *Royalist* branch.

Even if we could accept the equation of Independents with declining gentlemen, it would not help us to explain the civil war. For when the
40 war began the men in control at Westminster were not those whom we call Independents, and certainly not declining gentlemen; they were great peers like Warwick, Essex, Manchester; Hampden, the richest commoner in England; Pym, government employee and treasurer of a City company; Holles, son of a gentleman rich enough to buy an earldom.
45 When the Five Members escaped from the King's attempt to arrest them in January 1642, they did not flee to the backwoods; they retired to the City of London, where they were warmly welcomed. The civil war might not have been won without the Independents, but they did not start it . . . .

Christopher Hill, *Puritanism and Revolution*, 1968, pp 17−21

Questions

a What main criticisms does Hill make of Trevor-Roper's *methods* as a historian? Explain why Hill puts so much value on the research of Mrs Keeler.

* *b* Why does Hill take Pride's Purge (line 13) as the significant moment for his analysis of the members of parliament?
* *c* Explain the meaning of the term 'recruiters' (lines 17 and 18), putting it into its historical context.
  d For what main reasons does Hill reject Trevor-Roper's theory (i) that the Independents were made up of declining gentry (ii) that the declining gentry started the Civil War?
* *e* Write briefly on the contribution of (i) Vane (ii) Hesilrige (line 23) to the events of this period.

4 Hexter: Military Decline of the Aristocracy

Instead of statistics, Trevor-Roper offers us a brief but brilliant sketch of his conception of the role of the 'mere' or declining gentry in the politics and society of England from the age of Elizabeth to the Restoration. That this perdurable and undistinguished group was at large in England
5 between 1540 and 1640 is evident . . . . So far, what Trevor-Roper has to say seems most plausible. But rather often he goes beyond these plausibilities to broad though somewhat vague assertions. There are, he seems to indicate, really only two kinds of gentry – the fat courtly gentry and the depressed country gentry. The Great Rebellion thus becomes 'the
10 rising of the poor country gentry against the office-holders'. The Independents, who are mere gentry, convert the crisis of 1640 'from a series of political manoeuvres into civil war and social revolution'. It is they 'who more than any others made the Great Rebellion'.
   At this point the scope of Trevor-Roper's generalising brings one to an
15 abrupt halt; for it certainly goes beyond the evidence. In the first place most of the Independents were *not* gentry, either rising or declining. And however well the policy of the Independents may have mirrored their psyche, most of the declining gentry were *not* Independents. The gentry of the North and West, regions that provided such superior facilities for
20 going to pot on a stagnant rent roll, seem to have been predominantly Royalist. Moreover, a considerable number of the squires who sat in the Long Parliament, both Royalist and Roundheads, were in quite comfortable circumstances. They were neither overstuffed court gentry, nor bankrupt mere gentry, but substantial, fully solvent, country
25 gentry . . . .
   Recent investigation seems to show that, without the benefit of either demesne farming or court favour, from the 1580s on, the large landlords may have been doing very well for themselves. Around the 1580s the land market began to boom, and it seems to have continued to boom for
30 the next half century . . . . On the whole, a general increase in land values is likely to be most profitable in gross to the men who have the most land to profit from – that is, to the very segment of the landed class which both Tawney and Trevor-Roper have consigned to economic debility . . . .

35   We are still left with the problem that started Tawney on his
quest . . . . Why at this particular juncture did the 'country' find its
leadership in social strata beneath the top? Why among the gentry rather
than among the nobility? . . . Among the quotations from contemporaries on which he relies, there are several that point clearly to a line of
40   enquiry that he disregards. Now these men seem to be saying much the
same thing about the noble magnates; but what they are saying is not that
the nobles are bankrupt, or even much poorer than they used to be. They
are saying very emphatically that *the magnates do not directly control arms
and men as they once did*, that the old relation between high status or great
45   landed wealth and a great military following no longer subsists. On the
face of it, these observations direct our attention not to the economy but
to the organisation of armed forces. And if we follow their leading, we
discover that in the century and a half between Henry vi and the death of
Elizabeth there was indeed a transformation in the structure of England's
50   military reserve. In the middle of the 15th century, the larger part of the
battle-ready military reserve was made up of the retinues of the
magnates . . . . Most fee'd retainers were bound to come at the call of
their lord, prepared to fight under his command and in his quarrels. In
return, besides fee and livery, the magnate gave his follower
55   'goodlordship'. . . .
    At the end of the 16th century the bare form of the retaining system
survived; but it was a mere shell, a feeble shadow of its former self. The
squirearchy no longer rose in arms at the behest of the great lords,
although for show they might ride about the country in some personage's
60   train. In 1628 Parliament repealed almost every statute passed during the
preceding two hundred and fifty years to regulate, control, or suppress
the evil practices that flourished under the protection of the retaining
system . . . .
    Having lost their vocation for commanding retinues of armed squires,
65   the magnates had not yet found their vocation for commanding solid
phalanxes of borough members sitting in Parliament for the rotten and
pocket boroughs that magnates controlled. The result was a power
vacuum in England during the very years when a concurrence of fiscal,
constitutional, political and religious grievances evoked widespread
70   opposition to the Crown and made it necessary for the opposition to
achieve some measure of concerted action. Into the vacuum created by
the temporary incapacity of the magnates poured the country gentry –
not the brisk, hard-bitten small gentry of Professor Tawney nor yet the
mouldy, flea-bitten mere gentry of Professor Trevor-Roper, but the rich,
75   well-educated knights and squires who sat in the Parliaments of James i
and Charles i . . . . It is not an accident that when at last the opposition
rallied under one 'overmighty' subject, that subject for the first time in the
annals of England was not a great territorial magnate but a substantial
squire, a House of Commons man, John Pym.
    J. H. Hexter, 'Storm over the Gentry', *Encounter* (May 1958)
    pp 27–8, 32–4

Questions

a   In what way does Hexter criticise Trevor-Roper's *methods* as a historian?

b   Which two of Trevor-Roper's main arguments does Hexter dispute?

c   Explain why, according to Hexter, there was 'a power vacuum' (lines 67 and 68) in England during the years prior to 1640?

* d   What do you understand by the terms (i) 'demesne farming' (line 27) (ii) 'fee and livery' (line 54) (iii) 'goodlordship' (line 55)?

* e   What was the importance of John Pym (line 79) during the period 1640−43?

f   Having read these four extracts in the debate, do you feel that any of the theories concerning the gentry and the aristocracy are now acceptable?

IV Assessments of Oliver Cromwell

Introduction

Before the Restoration, historians who wrote accounts of the Civil War and Interregnum tended to look favourably on Oliver Cromwell. Some, indeed, wrote 'official' histories like the *History of the Parliament of England* by Thomas May (1647). Some, like John Rushworth (Cromwell's former Secretary) in his *Historical Collections* (1659), wrote out of loyalty to a person. Others wrote out of loyalty to the parliamentarian cause – like Joshua Sprigge in *Anglia Rediva* (1647) and John Vicars in *England's Parliamentarie Chronicle* (1646).

This emphasis changed dramatically in 1660. During the remaining years of the seventeenth century Cromwell was written about almost exclusively by his enemies. A great flood of royalist literature swept on to the market extolling the merits of Charles I and condemning the vices of Cromwell. This was typified by the work of James Heath, who had shared exile with Charles II. His *Flagellum: Or The Life and Death, Birth and Burial of Oliver Cromwell, The Late Usurper* (1663) became something of a standard royalist textbook for the period. Presbyterians like Denzil Holles in his *Memoirs* (1699) and Republicans like Edmund Ludlow in his *Memoirs* (1698) also denounced the treachery, ambition and hypocrisy of the man they had once respected. Even a puritan chaplain to the army like Richard Baxter found that Cromwell had given way to the temptation of power (*Reliquiae Baxterianae* (1696)). It took the earl of Clarendon (Charles II's Secretary of State) to discover that, amid undoubted wickedness, Cromwell nevertheless possessed some redeeming features. This verdict was reached in his majestic *History of the Rebellion* (1702).

Even though the writers of the eighteenth century were not involved in personal invective against Cromwell, their histories were largely based on the royalist chronicles which were often taken at their face value. It is true that he was no longer thought of as a complete villain, but his sincerity and motives were still very much in doubt (e.g. Smollet, *History of England*; Hume, *History of Great Britain*).

The nineteenth century witnessed a dramatic turn in the fortunes of Cromwell at the hands of historians. It is true that Victorian England with its early romanticism, its later imperialism and its more personal approach to religion saw much to admire in Cromwell. But the real impetus came in 1845 with the publication of Thomas Carlyle's *The Letters and Speeches of Oliver Cromwell*. This largely exploded the myth of Cromwell's hypocrisy and showed him to be at least a man of sincere Christian convictions. The rediscovery and use of original documents was further extended by the work of the German historian Von Ranke with his 'scientific history'. This more scholarly approach, from which Cromwell's reputation benefited enormously, reached its climax with the publication of *The History of the Commonwealth and Protectorate* by S. R. Gardiner in 1897. His conclusion was that Cromwell must be considered as 'the greatest and most powerful Englishman of all time'.

The twentieth century has continued to admire the life and work of Cromwell, though with some reservations. The Victorian background of religion and empire has given way to contemporary concern for material comforts and the state of the economy. Recent historians have therefore been more interested to assess Cromwell's concrete achievements in social, economic and political affairs than to discuss his hypocrisy or even his ideals. But, as C. V. Wedgwood wrote in 1973, 'his reputation changes – as it will continue to change – with the moral and political climate of the living world'.

1 James Heath: Verdict of a Royalist Exile

From this haughty confidence he was invited to call another Parliament, and to assume from thence the long awaited result of his ambition, the Crown Imperial of England . . . . This was the critical time, and the very juncture of his accomplishment of all his projections upon the Crown,
5 which now seemed to court his brows by the complemental tender of a Parliament so picked and culled to his purpose. But it pleased God, to rescue the honour and majesty of England, from the profaneness of his temples, by some sudden emergent dangers, and suspicions he raised in his breast . . . .
10 This Kingdom was now almost stupefied and tired out with the struggling against his government and domination, when it pleased God to call him to an account of all that mischief he had perpetrated . . . . He died on Friday the 3rd of September at 3 of the clock in the afternoon, though diverse rumours were spread, that he was carried away in the
15 Tempest the day before: His body being opened and embalmed his milt was found full of corruption and filth, which was so strong and stinking, that after the Corpse were embalmed and filled with aromatic odours, and wrapped in cloth, six double, in an inner sheet of lead, and a strong wooden coffin, yet the filth broke through them all, and raised such a
20 noisome stink, that they were forced to bury him out of hand; but his

name and memory stinks worse.

James Heath, *Flagellum: Or The Life and Death, Birth and Burial of Oliver Cromwell, The Late Usurper*, 1663

Questions

a Which parts of this extract represent (i) historical fact (ii) biased personal opinion?

* *b* Which of Cromwell's parliaments is referred to in line 1? Explain what is meant by 'complemental tender' (line 5) and 'picked and culled to his purpose' (line 6).

* *c* What were the 'sudden emergent dangers, and suspicions' which Heath mentions (line 8)?

2 Richard Baxter: Verdict of an Army Chaplain

Never was man highlier extolled, and never man was baselier reported of and vilified than this man. No (mere) man was better and worse spoken of than he, according as men's interests led their judgments. The soldiers and sectaries most highly magnified him till he began to seek the crown and
5 the establishment of his family . . . . The Royalists abhorred him as a most perfidious hypocrite, and the Presbyterians thought him little better in his management of public matters.

If after so many others I may speak my opinion of him, I think that, having been a prodigal in his youth and afterward changed to a zealous
10 religiousness, he meant honestly in the main, and was pious and conscionable in the main course of his life till prosperity and success corrupted him . . . . With their successes the hearts both of captain and soldiers secretly rise both in pride and expectation; and the familiarity of many honest erroneous men (Anabaptists, Antinomians, etc.) withall
15 began quickly to corrupt their judgments. Hereupon Cromwell's general religious zeal giveth way to the power of that ambition, which still increaseth as his successes do increase . . . . He meaneth well in all this at the beginning, and thinketh he doth all for the safety of the godly and the public good, but not without an eye to himself . . . .
20 Having thus forced his conscience to justify all his cause (the cutting off the King, the setting up himself and his adherents, the pulling down the parliament and the Scots), he thinketh that the end being good and necessary, the necessary means cannot be bad . . . . He seemed exceeding open-hearted, by a familiar rustic-affected carriage (especially to his
25 soldiers in sporting with them); but he thought secrecy a virtue, and dissimulation no vice, and simulation − that is, in plain English, a lie − or perfidiousness to be a tolerable fault in a case of necessity.

Richard Baxter, *Reliquiae Baxterianae*, 1696

Questions

a   Why have opinions varied so greatly on Cromwell's worth?

b   Why, according to Baxter, did Cromwell's character change?

c   Explain from your knowledge of the period why both the Royalists and the Presbyterians thought that Cromwell was a 'perfidious hypocrite' (line 6).

*   d   Explain what you understand by (i) sectaries (line 4), (ii) Anabaptists (line 14).

*   e   State precisely which historical events are referred to in lines 20–22: 'the cutting off the King, the setting up himself and his adherents, the pulling down the parliament and the Scots'.

3   Edmund Ludlow: Verdict of a Republican

Having seen our cause betrayed, and the most solemn promises that could be made to the asserters of it, openly violated, I departed from my native country. And hoping that my retirement may protect me from the rage and malice of my enemies, I cannot think it a misspending of some part of
5   my leisure, to employ it in setting down the most remarkable counsels and actions of the parties engaged in the late Civil War . . . .

Thus the enemy by the blessing of God upon the counsels of the Parliament, and endeavours of their armies, was everywhere dispersed and conquered, and the nation likely to attain in a short time that measure
10   of happiness which humane things are capable of, when by the ambition of one man the hopes and expectations of all good men were disappointed, and the people robbed of that liberty which they had contended for at the expense of so much blood and treasure.

General Cromwell had long been suspected by wise and good men; but
15   he had taken such care to form and mould the army to his humour and interests, that he had filled all places either with his own creatures, or with such as hoped to share with him in the sovereignty, and removed those who foreseeing his design, had either the courage or honesty to oppose him in it. His pernicious intentions did not discover themselves openly till
20   after the battle at Worcester, which in one of his letters to the Parliament he called The Crowning Victory . . . . In a word so much was he elevated with that success, that Mr. Hugh Peters, as he since told me, took so much notice of it, as to say in confidence to a friend upon the road in his return from Worcester, that Cromwell would make himself King . . . .
25   But either the General's ambition was so great, that he could not forbear ascending the throne till the time limited by the Parliament for their sitting was expired, or his fears hastened him to the accomplishment of his design . . . . Certain it is that he vehemently desired to be rid of this parliament that had performed such great things . . . . Of this Cromwell
30   was very sensible, as well as of their great skill and experience in the management of public affairs, and of the good esteem they had acquired

amongst the most discerning part of the nation, and therefore was very desirous to lay them aside with as little noise as might be . . . . This made him join with Major-General Harrison, being confident that when he had used him and his party to dissolve the present Government, he could crush both him and them at his pleasure. And though it was no difficult matter to discover this, yet those poor, deluded, however well-meaning men, would not believe it.

> The Memoirs of Edmund Ludlow, 1698, Vol I, pp 9, 343–4, 349–50

Questions

* *a* In what ways had the cause which Ludlow supported been 'betrayed' by Cromwell and his followers (line 1)?
  b What characteristics does Ludlow see in Cromwell?
* *c* Explain the historical significance of the battle of Worcester (line 20).
* *d* Which parliament is referred to in the final paragraph? Do you agree that it 'had performed such great things' (line 29)?
* *e* Who was Major-General Harrison? What was 'his party' (lines 34 and 35)? How did Cromwell 'use' them now and 'crush' them later (lines 35 and 36)?
  f How objective do you think is this assessment by Ludlow?

4 Denzil Holles: Verdict of a Presbyterian

Well, they carried it (the Covenant), and to work they go, bearing it very fair to the Scots, and, with their help, they had recovered and cleared the North, and obtained that great Victory at *Marston-Moor*, in July 1644, which without them they would never have done. And, however Lieutenant-General *Cromwell* had the impudence and boldness to assume much of the honour of that victory to himself, or rather, *Herod*-like, to suffer others to magnify him and adore him for it (for I can scarce believe that he should be so impudent as to give it out himself, so conscious as he must be of his own base cowardliness) those who did the principal service that day were Major-General *Lesley*, who commanded the Scots Horse, Major-General *Crawford*, who was Major-General to the Earl of Manchester's Brigade, and Sir *Thomas Fairfax*, who, under his Father, commanded the Northern Brigade. But my friend *Cromwell* had neither part nor lot in the business: For I have several times heard it from Crawford's own mouth that, when the whole Army at *Marston-Moor* was in a fair possibility to be utterly routed, and a great part of it was running, he saw a Body of Horse of that Brigade standing-still, and, to his seeming, doubtful which way to charge, backward or forward, when he came up to them in great passion, reviling them with the name of Poltroons and Cowards, and asked them if they would stand still and see the day lost? Whereupon *Cromwell* shewed himself, and, in a pitiful voice,

said 'Major-General, what shall I do?' he (begging pardon for what he had said, not knowing he was there, towards whom he knew his distance, as to his Superior Officer) told him, 'Sir, if you charge not, all is lost';
Cromwell answered, 'that he was wounded, and was not able to charge' (his great wound being a little burn in his neck by the accidental going-off, behind him, of one of his soldiers pistols), then *Crawford* desired him to go off the field, and sending one away with him led them on himself; which was not the duty of his place, and as little for *Cromwell's* honour, as it proved to be much for the advancement of his and his Party's pernicious designs. This I have but by relation: yet I easily believe it upon the credit of the reporter, who was a man of honour, that was not ashamed or afraid to publish it in all places . . . . And something I can deliver of him upon my own knowledge, which assures me that that Man is as errant a Coward, as he is notoriously perfidious, ambitious and hypocritical. This was his base keeping out of the Field at *Keinton* Battle; where he, with his troop of horse, came not in; impudently and ridiculously affirming, the day after, that he had been all that day seeking the Army and place of fight, though his Quarters were but at a Village near hand, whence he could not find his way, nor be directed by his ear, though the ordnance was heard (as I have been credibly informed) 20 or 30 miles off; so that certainly he is far from being the Man he is taken for.

> *Memoirs of Denzil Lord Holles*, 1699

Questions

a Pick out the phrases and words which indicate that this writer was personally hostile to Cromwell.

* *b* Which 'three nations' had Cromwell subdued (line 17)? Explain from why he was hostile to Cromwell.

c What is Holles attempting to do in this extract? What questions ought we to ask about the reliability of his evidence?

* *d* What was the historical importance of the battle of Marston Moor (line 3)? How important was the part played by the Scots?

* *e* Write briefly about the importance of Sir Thomas Fairfax during this period (line 12).

5 Earl of Clarendon: Verdict of a Constitutional Royalist

He was one of those men *quos vituperare ne inimici quidem possunt nisi ut simul laudent* [whom not even their enemies can curse unless it is to praise them at the same time]; for he could never have done half that mischief without great parts of courage and industry and judgment. And he must have had a wonderful understanding in the natures and humours of men, and as great a dexterity in the applying them, who from a private and obscure birth (though of a good family), without interest of estate,

alliance or friendships, could raise himself to such a height, and compound and knead such opposite and contradictory tempers, hu-
10 mours, and interests, into a consistence that contributed to his designs and to their own destruction; . . . Without doubt, no man with more wickedness ever attempted anything, or brought to pass what he desired more wickedly, more in the face and contempt of religion and moral honesty, yet wickedness as great as his could never have accomplished
15 those trophies without the assistance of a great spirit, an admirable circumspection and sagacity, and a most magnanimous resolution . . . .

To reduce three nations, which perfectly hated him, to an entire obedience to all his dictates; to awe and govern those nations by an army that was indevoted to him and wished his ruin; was an instance of a very
20 prodigious address. But his greatness at home was but a shadow of the glory he had abroad. It was hard to discover which feared him most, France, Spain or the Low Countries, where his friendship was current at the value he put upon it. And as they did all sacrifice their honour and their interest to his pleasure, so there is nothing he could have demanded
25 that either of them would have denied him . . . .

He was not a man of blood, and totally declined Machiavell's method, which prescribes upon any alteration of a government, as a thing absolutely necessary, to cut off all the heads of those, and extirpate their families, who are friends to the old (one). And it was confidently
30 reported, that in the council of officers it was more than once proposed that there might be a general massacre of all the royal party, as the only expedient to secure the government, but Cromwell would never consent to it; it may be, out of too much contempt of his enemies. In a word, as he had all the wickednesses against which damnation is denounced and for
35 which hell-fire is prepared, so he had some virtues which have caused the memory of some men in all ages to be celebrated; and he will be looked upon by posterity as a brave bad man.

Clarendon, *History of the Rebellion*, 1702, Vol. xv, pp 147, 152, 156

Questions

a   What *good* qualities does Clarendon see in Cromwell?

* b   Which 'three nations' had Cromwell subdued (line 17)? Explain from your historical knowledge how he had achieved this.

* c   Is there any historical evidence to suggest that Cromwell's army 'was indevoted to him and wished his ruin' (line 19)?

* d   Outline briefly Cromwell's main dealings with France, Spain and the Low Countries (line 22). Do you agree that his foreign policy was full of 'glory' (line 21)?

* e   What historical evidence is there to support Clarendon's view that Cromwell was not Machiavellian in his methods (line 26)?

6 Thomas Carlyle: No Hypocrisy

These authentic utterances of the man Oliver himself – I have gathered them from far and near; fished them up from the foul Lethean quagmires where they lay buried; I have washed, or endeavoured to wash them clean from foreign stupidities; and the world shall now see them in their own shape. Working for long years in those unspeakable Historic Provinces, it becomes more and more apparent to one, That this man Oliver Cromwell was, as the popular fancy represents him the soul of the Puritan Revolt . . . . And then farther, altogether contrary to popular fancy, it becomes apparent that this Oliver was not a man of falsehoods, but a man of truths; whose words do carry a meaning with them, and above all others of that time are worth considering . . . . An earnest man, I apprehend, may gather from these words of Oliver's, were there even no other evidence, that the character of Oliver, and of the Affairs he worked in, is much the reverse of that mad jumble of 'hypocrisies' etc. etc., which at present passes current as such . . . . Even if false, these words, authentically spoken and written by the chief actor in the business, must be of prime moment for understanding of it. These are the words this man found suitablest to represent the Things themselves, around him, and in him, of which we seek a History . . . .

To dwell on or criticise the particular Biographies of Cromwell would profit us little . . . . Of Cromwell's actual biography, from these and from all books and sources, there is extremely little to be known. It is from his own words, as I have ventured to believe, from his own Letters and Speeches well read, that the world may first obtain some dim glimpse of the actual Cromwell, and see him darkly face to face.

Thomas Carlyle, *Letters and Speeches of Oliver Cromwell*, 1845

Questions

a How important a source are the writings and speeches of a major character such as Cromwell? How reliable are they as historical evidence?

b Why was Carlyle so critical of previous biographies of Cromwell?

7 C. H. Firth: No Dishonesty

Either as a soldier or as a statesman Cromwell was far greater than any Englishman of his time, and he was both soldier and statesman in one. We must look to Caesar or Napoleon to find a parallel for this union of high political and military ability in one man. Cromwell was not as great a man as Caesar or Napoleon, and he played his part on a smaller stage, but he 'bestrode the narrow world' of Puritan England 'like a colossus' . . . .

Cromwell's victories, however, were due to his own military genius even more than to the quality of his troops. The most remarkable thing in

his military career is that it began so late. Most successful generals have
10 been trained to arms from their youth, but Cromwell was forty-three
years old before he heard a shot fired or set a squadron in the field. How
was it, people often ask, that an untrained country gentleman beat
soldiers who had learnt their trade under the most famous captains in
Europe? The answer is that Cromwell had a natural aptitude for war, and
15 that circumstances were singularly favourable to its rapid and full
development . . . .

It is plain, however, that Cromwell was a statesman of a different order
from most. Religious rather than political principles guided his action,
and his political ideals were the direct outcome of his creed . . . . For his
20 own part, Cromwell believed in 'dispensations' rather than 'revelations'.
Since all things which happened in the world were determined by God's
will, the statesman's problem was to discover the hidden purpose which
underlay events . . . . With Cromwell, in every political crisis this
attempt to interpret the meaning of events was part of the mental process
25 which preceded action. As it was difficult to be sure what that meaning
was, he was often slow to make up his mind, preferring to watch events a
little longer and to allow them to develop in order to get more light. This
slowness was not the result of indecision, but a deliberate suspension of
judgment. When his mind was made up there was no hesitation, no
30 looking back; he struck with the same energy in politics as in war.

This system of being guided by events had its dangers. Political
inconsistency is generally attributed to dishonesty, and Cromwell's
inconsistency was open and palpable. One year he was foremost in
pressing for an agreement with the King, another foremost in bringing
35 him to the block; now all for a republic, now all for a government with
some element of monarchy in it. His changes of policy were so sudden
that even his friends found it difficult to excuse them. A pamphleteer,
who believed in the honesty of Cromwell's motives, lamented his
'sudden engaging for and sudden turning from things', as arguing
40 inconstancy and want of foresight. Moreover the effect of this inconsistency was aggravated by the violent zeal with which Cromwell threw
himself into the execution of each new policy . . . .

Cromwell remained throughout his life too much the champion of a
party to be accepted as a national hero by later generations, but in serving
45 his Cause he served his country too. No English ruler did more to shape
the future of the land he governed, none showed more clearly in his acts
the 'plain heroic magnitude of mind'.

C. H. Firth, *Oliver Cromwell and the Rule of the Puritans in England,*
1900

Questions

a How do you measure greatness in history?
* *b* Why was Cromwell's military achievement so 'remarkable' (line 8)?
Explain why 'circumstances were singularly favourable' (line 15) to

the development of his natural skill.

* c From your historical knowledge, give examples of occasions when 'religious rather than political principles' guided Cromwell's actions (line 18).

d Explain the difference between 'dispensations' and 'revelations' (line 20). Why is it wrong to accuse Cromwell of indecision?

* e Give a historical example of a 'political crisis' in Cromwell's career which followed the pattern described by Firth (lines 23 and 30).

f How does Firth answer the charges of dishonesty made against Cromwell by critics like Baxter and Ludlow? (See also extracts 2 and 3.)

8 C. V. Wedgwood: No Personal Ambition

I wrote this short account of Cromwell in 1939 . . . . The present version is revised and in parts much re-written. In the 34 years which have gone by since it first appeared, massive research has been done on the Stuart period, and new material has come to light. Our knowledge has
5 been broadened and enriched by the opening up of new veins of enquiry and the re-working of older ones.

Yet the personality of Cromwell remains enigmatic and his reputation changes – as it will continue to change – with the moral and political climate of the living world. In 1939 the shadow of the European
10 dictatorships darkened his image and historians who still clung to the older liberal interpretation of him as a national hero in the evolution of English liberty were thrown on to the defensive. They were often concerned above all to show that the Great Protector had nothing in common with the Führer or the Duce. This produced a rather negative
15 interpretation, emphasising what Cromwell was *not*, rather than what he *was* . . . . Some writers, on the other hand, thought that they could detect parallels between Cromwell and contemporary dictators . . . . Even in the tercentenary year of 1958 popular comment still emphasised Cromwell the Dictator above all else.
20 The atmosphere has changed. If Cromwell is not quite a national hero, he is generally recognised as a great figure in our history, the soldier–statesman who put an end to civil war, restored peace at home and respect abroad. But his career and character remain controversial.

He was hard to understand even in his own day. How much harder
25 then is it for us to reach the heart of his mystery, since we must approach him through a mist of prejudices, beliefs and received opinions very different from those of his own time . . . .

His actions, in crisis, whether on the battle-field, in Parliament or at the Council table, show a clear and bold judgment; but he was not good at
30 analysing or presenting the reasons behind his actions. Prayer helped him towards all his considered decisions, and the insights which were then vouchsafed to him he took for direct revelation . . . .

In his years of power there is no evidence of any personal pleasure or even gratification at his own greatness: no evidence that ambition had been satisfied. Can this be taken as evidence that personal ambition was never a motive with him? I am inclined to think so.

He felt the burden but did not enjoy the rewards of his position. His personal joys and griefs came from his private feelings – grief for the loss of friends, for the fatal illness of his beloved daughter, and joy – more rarely – at moments of relaxation and family gaiety. As protector he appeared, in spite of his power at home and prestige abroad, a sad and heavily burdened man.

C. V. Wedgwood, *Oliver Cromwell*, 1973, pp 119–22

Questions

a   Why do historians find it necessary to revise their original opinions?
* b   What 'new veins of enquiry' have been opened up during recent years by historians working on this period?
c   Explain how a historical character's reputation can be changed by changes in the 'moral and political climate of the living world' (lines 8 and 9).
d   Why is it difficult to understand Cromwell?
e   Why does Wedgwood dismiss the charge of personal ambition against Cromwell?

V Civil War and the Local Community

Introduction

Local history has provided one of the most fruitful areas of study in the twentieth century for research into the English Civil War. Whereas previous authors had concentrated on presenting a straight narrative of military events in the locality, Mary Coate set a new pattern in the 1930s by also examining the nature of the local community (*Cornwall in the Great Civil War and Interregnum*). Since then, stimulated by the opening of County Record Offices and by the desire to produce case-studies for examination in the Gentry Controversy, historians have continued to explore the relationship between national events and local society.

The documents in this section chiefly concern the city of Bath and the surrounding area of north-east Somerset. In 1642 Bath was a prosperous walled city of some two thousand people. Its livelihood was based on a lucrative cloth trade and its fame as a health resort. From the outset of the Civil War the community declared its vigorous support for parliament (see document 2). But how far was this decision influenced by the wishes of three powerful local leaders – John Ashe (the greatest clothier in the Kingdom), Alexander Popham (the wealthy M.P. for Bath) and William Prynne (a nationally famous pamphleteer)? How great was the city's real involvement in the war? How quickly did disillusionment set in? How seriously was ordinary everyday life disrupted by local hostilities, which included royalist occupation, the battle of Landsdown and siege by the New Model Army? How severe was the conflict between loyalty to the state and loyalty to the local community?

Further Reading

A. M. Everitt, *The Community of Kent and the Great Rebellion* (Leicester UP, 1966)

A. M. Everitt, *The Local Community and the Great Rebellion* (Historical Association, 1969)

Clive Holmes, *The Eastern Association in the English Civil War* (Cambridge, 1974)

David Underdown, *Somerset in the Civil War and Interregnum* (David &
Charles, 1973)

Roger Howell, *Newcastle-upon-Tyne and the Puritan Revolution* (Oxford,
1967)

Valerie Pearl, *London and the Outbreak of the Puritan Revolution* (Oxford,
1961)

1 Local versus National Loyalty

The allegiance of the provincial gentry to the community of their native
shire is one of the basic facts of English history in the seventeenth and
eighteenth centuries. Though the sense of national identity had been
increasing since the early Tudors, so too had the sense of county identity,
and the latter was normally, I believe, the more powerful sentiment in
1640–60. There were many factors in the development of regional
loyalty: the growth of county administration, the development of county
instututitions, the expanding wealth of the local gentry, their increasing
tendency to intermarriage, their growing interest in local history and
legal custom, the rise of the county towns as social, cultural, and
administrative centres: these and many other elements entered into the
rise of what Namier once called the 'county commonwealths' of
England.

In some respects the Civil War period, by greatly adding to the
complexity and volume of local government, increased this sense of
county awareness . . . . Despite the well-known fact that many gentry
attended the universities and some of the wealthier families spent part of
the year in London, the vast majority of country gentry passed most of
their lives within a few miles of their native manor-house, in a circle often
as limited as that of their tenants and labourers. The brief years at the
university and Inns of Court were no more than an interlude, principally
designed to fit them out for their functions as justices, squires, and
landlords in their own county . . . .

In 1640, however, local attachments were, if anything, becoming
deeper rather than more superficial. For this reason the Civil War was not
simply a struggle between gallant Cavaliers and psalm-singing
Roundheads . . . . This does not mean that most English people were
indifferent to the political problems of the time, but that their loyalties
were polarised around different ideals. For them, bounded as they so
often were by local horizons, a more urgent problem was the conflict
between loyalty to the nation and loyalty to the county community. This
division cut across the conventional divisions, like a geological fault. The
unwillingness of most people to forgo the independence of their shire and
admit that allegiance to the Kingdom as a whole must override it was
certainly one of the reasons why the Civil War was so long drawn
out . . . .

In a world with poor communications and no country newspapers it was inevitable that most people should be chiefly concerned with the fortunes of their local community. It was not that they never heard any national news, but that they were not *continuously* preoccupied with it as we are today. There were other matters of more immediate concern, and most people lived too near the bone to spare much time for political speculation.

For these reasons few political actions in the seventeenth century could be determined by unfettered idealism, or by abstract principle alone. They had to work themselves out in a complex and intractable provincial world. Every decision, every loyalty was shaped, not so much by a fiat of government, as by the whole network of local society: by all the pressures of personal influence, family connection, ancient amity, local pride, religious sentiment, economic necessity, and a dozen other matters, now often very difficult to track down . . . .

How much were ordinary people really affected by the events of the Great Rebellion? The present writer is gradually coming to the conclusion that we may have exaggerated the impact of the war itself upon daily life in the provinces. In the Midlands, of course, country people could not fail at times to be conscious of the fighting, and for some of them – the people of Leicester, for instance, on a May evening in 1645 – it brought horror and tragedy. Yet it would be misleading to suppose that daily life was *continuously* disrupted by fighting, even in the Midlands. The Great Rebellion was far from being a total war as we understand that term.

When we read of the uproar occasioned in 1643 by Lord Northampton's seizure of a train of carriers' waggons at Daventry, drawn by 57 horses on their journey from Cheshire to London, we need to remember, not only the outrage itself, but the fact that normally speaking these carriers' trains must have continued to reach their destination, otherwise there would have been no occasion for the outcry . . . .

There is, of course, no need to minimise the impact of the Civil War upon seventeenth-century England. Its consequences for provincial society were obviously far-reaching. But we also need to see the Rebellion as one of a succession of problems to which society at the time was peculiarly vulnerable. The recurrent problems of harvest failure, and the malnutrition and disease that often followed in its wake, were, for the most English people, more serious and more persistent than the tragic but temporary upheaval of the Civil War . . . . During the seventeenth century as a whole every fourth harvest, on the average, fell seriously short of basic requirements, and in some decades several successive years showed a marked deficiency. Those who lived through the Civil War and Commonwealth period, for example, suffered no fewer than ten harvest failures within the space of fifteen or sixteen years, and in two years (1649–50 and 1661–2) the general price-level of foodstuffs was more than 50 per cent above normal. This kind of situation affected every class in the country, and for hundreds of thousands of labourers, yeomen,

85 craftsmen, and traders it might well mean ruin . . . .

Their experiences certainly go some way to explain that latent intransigence of the provincial world which, in the last resort, was one of the principal factors in the failure of both Charles I and Cromwell. For if you have been engaged for centuries in hand-to-hand warfare with the
90 forces of nature, you naturally develop a certain dumb obstinacy towards the world at large – and not least towards the strange doings of princes and protectors.

> A. M. Everitt, *The Local Community and the Great Rebellion*, 1969, pp 5–6, 8, 23–8

Questions

a   What main reasons does Everitt give in this extract as a whole to explain why most people were 'chiefly concerned with the fortunes of their local community' (lines 38 and 39) rather than of the nation as a whole?

b   Why does Everitt feel that the impact of the war on the daily lives of ordinary people was not as great as was perhaps previously believed?

c   In what practical ways would 'loyalty to the nation' (line 31) conflict with 'loyalty to the county community' during the period of the Civil War?

* d   Explain how the people of Leicester experienced 'horror and tragedy' (line 58) on a May evening in 1645. What was the main sequel to this?

* e   Suggest reasons for the increased sense of *national* identity 'since the early Tudors' (line 4).

* f   Explain what 'county administration' (line 7) consisted of in seventeenth-century England. In what practical ways did the Civil War add to the 'volume of local government' (line 15)?

2   Local Zeal

. . . and thither [Chewton Mendip] came unto us all the Trained Bands of that quarter of the Shire, and especially Master Popham's Regiment compleate in number, nay doubled twice over by means of volunteers, who came best armed ˙. . . . Many had no more weapons but their
5 swords, yet all came to shew their affections to the King and Parliament, and to oppose with the hazard of their lives the Lord Marquesse of Hertford and his company with their Commission of Array . . . . The company was put into order but with much adoe for want of expert souldiers and commanders, which done the souldiers (although they had
10 neither meate nor drinke) could not be stayed but would march over the Hill, which was neere foure miles, until they came in sight of Wells . . . . By this time the day was neere spent and victualls we had none nor could we get any upon the suddaine, yet such was the courage and resolution of our Company, that after they had planted their ordnance

15 they would not depart that place, but lay all that night upon the hill,
fasting and in the cold, and spent the time in prayers and singing of
Psalms. Sir John Horner and Master Alexander Popham with his two
valiant brothers, and Sir John Horner's youngest sonne, with many other
young Gentlemen, Captaines and others, lay all that night in their Armes
20 upon Fursbushes in the Open Fields amidst the Camp, the old Knight
often saying that his Furs-Bed was the best he lay upon. It was very much
to be admired that the Spirits and resolutions of so great a company, and
men so tenderly bred could be kept up to that night, as to indure so much
hunger and cold. But such was the love and affections of all the country
25 within eight and ten miles distance, that by the next morning daylight
they sent in such provision of all sorts in waynes, carts and on horses, that
this great company had sufficient and to spare, both for breakfast and
dinner, and would not take a penny for it, nay many did carry home
againe their provisions, for want of Company to eate it.
30 John Ashe, *A Perfect Relation from the Committee of Sommersetshire*,
     1642

Certaine newes also came this day, that Sir Arthur Aston [the royalist
Governor of Reading] had siezed on seven cart-loades, one waine-loade,
and 24 hourse-loades of broad fine cloth, amounting in the whole unto
35 380 clothes, and that in many of the packs were found some *Belts* and
Bandoleers, and great store of *Match*, and a considerable summe of
Money. All which were sent towards London from one Mr. Ashe, the
greatest *Clothier* in the Kingdome, as it is conceived, but of so turbulent a
spirit and so pernicious a practicer in the maintaining and fomenting of
40 this Rebellion, that he stands excepted by His Majesty amongst some
others, out of His Majesties generall pardon for the County of
Sommerset.
     Mercurius Aulicus, 16 March, 1643

Questions

a What evidence in the first extract suggests that the army in question
   was largely unprepared for the outbreak of civil war?
b What evidence is there to suggest that the muster was the result of
   popular local feeling?
* c How important, do you feel, was the influence of Ashe and Popham
   on the local rising? Give reasons. Why did they have more contact
   with London than most local people?
* d Explain what you understand by (i) 'the Trained Bands' (line 1)
   (ii) 'Commission of Array' (line 7) (iii) 'the Committee of
   Sommersetshire' (see the 1642 title of Ashe's account)
   (iv) 'Bandoleers' (line 36).
* e Why were textile areas like north-east Somerset more likely to be
   parliamentarian in sympathy?
f Ashe's narrative was reprinted in pamphlet form from a letter he

wrote to the Speaker. *Mercurius Aulicus* was a royalist newspaper. Assess the reliability of these as historical sources with reference to these extracts.

3   Local Losses

An account of all money, plate, armes that were taxed, assessed or sequestered and free quarter given since the beginning of the warre; taken before the commissioners att Bath, June 2nd 1646.

Newton St. Loe .

5   . . . 5 loads of hay for Sir William Waller's Troopers 2 for Sir
Arthur Haslerigge's troopers 1 for Mr. John Ashe's own
horse   £5.0.0.
. . . 2 horses by command of Sir William Waller at
Roundway Hill   £8.0.0.

10   *Combhay*
. . . Captain Sanderson one troupe of horse, and men in
number 60, 2 weeks and odde dayes, constantly quartered beside ye dayly concourse of ye whole armie to our
village, dureinge Sr William Wallers being about Bath
15   downes and Odde downe   £42.0.0.
The same tyme his keepinge centre on ye Bathe downes,
spoyling our grounde ready for mowinge, besydes haie,
fytches, carrved to ye countrie to them, with exceedinge
spoyle and losse of sheepe to ye number of 80   £60.0.0.

20   *Norton St. Phillipes*
. . . Quartered Col. Alexandre Phopham Regement of ffoot
two dayes and two nights being 700 of them   £35.0.0.
Payd to Sir Will. Wallers quatre master generall for haye
and otes when they quartered at Bradfourd   £6.0.0.
25   . . . 2 horses set fourth to Sr William Waller for the use of the
state to carry the Ammunition from Bath and never
returned   £8.0.0.

1 plowe 3 dayes to Bristoll for the use of Coll. Burch   £1.0.0.

Charlescombe
30   . . . Sustayned losse by Sr William Waller's Army at the
fight at Lansdowne in hay, grass and wood to the value
of   £10.0.0.
. . . William Maynard's bill for bread, beare, hay and grasse
that was taken from him for the use of Sr. Wm. Waller
35   when he fought at Lansdowne   £5.5.6.
For bread, beare, barly, mault and other necessaries

taken for the use of Sr William Waller and for
quartering 5 troops   £9.9.6.
Public Record Office, S. P. 28. 175

Questions

a   Examine these claims made by villages around Bath for damage
sustained during the summer of 1643. In what ways did *farming* suffer
as a result of the presence of the army?

*   *b*   Bearing in mind Everitt's arguments in document 1, why would
prolonged military intrusion of the kind recorded here bring
inevitable personal suffering to local villagers?

c   How reliable do you consider these returns to be as historical sources?

*   *d*   Write briefly on the historical importance of (i) 'Sir William Waller'
(line 5) (ii) 'Sir Arthur Haslerigge' (line 6) (iii) 'Roundway Hill' (line
9) (iv) 'the fight at Lansdowne' (line 31).

4   Local Affairs

. . . Item to Mr Mynn Skoole master his stipend	£20.0.0.
. . . Item to the poore at Christmas in wood	£0.8.4.
. . . Item to the poore in Cole at Christmas	£2.8.0.
. . . Item to the poore of St. Johns Hospitall	£1.4.0.
5 . . . Item to the poore in Bread at Lent	£4.0.0.
. . . Item to Elianor Singer and Mary Ady for helpinge poore strangers at the Leapers Bath	£1.5.0.
. . . Item payd for mending the water course to the Cundict house	£2.15.0.
10 . . . Item payd for wood the 5th of November for banfiers	£5.6.
. . . Item payd for wood Coale and Candells for the Court of Guards	£1.10.0.
. . . Item payd to the Tyler and glasier for worke done at the Schoole house	£0.7.0.
15 . . . Item payd for Candells for the Queenes comminge to Towne	£0.6.8.
. . . Item payd to William Dolton for mendinge westgate	£0.2.6.
. . . Item payd for Bread and Beare for the freemen on Whit Munday	£0.1.6.
20 . . . Item payd for wood for Bonfiers by Mr. Mayors appoyntment	£0.6.0.
. . . Item payd to Mr. Masters for 2 Sarmons	£0.13.4.
. . . Item payd to Thomas Bullman for makeinge a hedge under the Burrowalls	£0.8.0.
25 . . . Item payd for a srowde and buringe of a stranger wch was drowned in the Kings Bathe	£0.3.0.

... Item payd for mendinge the gutters at the Towne
Hall   £0.1.6.
... Item payd for a stooke for the Buchers shambells   £0.3.0.
30 ... Item payd for wood Cole and Candells for the Princes
guards   £0.1.6.
... Item payd to John Beacon for his worke Done at the
Markett house   £1.15.0.
Bath Chamberlain's Accounts, October 1643 – October 1645

35 *Novem 1 1643.* Agreed that Mr. Hayward shall have stones out of the quarr
in the Common for 3d. a load he being at the charge of digging them and
carrying them from the lanes or Comon highway
Feb 12 1644. Agreed that 50.1: shalbe taken up for the buyinge of Ten
Barrels of Powder by the Cittie for the use of his Ma.ties Service
40 *ffeb 27 1644.* Agreed that Mr. Druce and Mr. Cole shall be Overseers of the
Comon for the next year
Agreed that Richard Riall shall be Scavenger for the next year
April 15 1644. William Baker elected Guide of the Cross Bath Susan Beker
Joane Speringe and ffranncis Snalyam elected Guides of the Cross Bath
45 *May 13 1644.* Agreed that a Rate shall be made through out the Cittie for
the gathering of 40.1: for prince Maurice
March 31 1645. Katherine Griffyn a decrepit old Maid servant to Mr.
Richard Chapman is admitted by generall consent into the Almeshouse
of the Blew gown for life
50 *April 18 1645.* Ordered that the Comon Groundes belonging to this
Cittie shall from henceforth be hayned only for hay and that no catle shall
be put therein till the hay be cut
October 13 1645. Ordered that all the Bathes within this Cittie shall every
day be drained at fower of the Clock in the afternoon and the doores to be
55 shutt and the Bathes to be stopped againe at Seaven that it may be full in
convenient time the next morning
ffeb 9 1646. Agreed that a peticion shall be preferred to the houses of
Parliament for release of ffree quarter
Bath Council Minute Book, 1643 – 6

Questions

a   What evidence is there in these documents to suggest that the
following aspects of normal everyday life were not completely
disrupted even during the period of Royalist occupation between 1643 and 1645 (i) agriculture (ii) religion (iii) education
(iv) trade (v) social and leisure activity (vi) charity (vii) routine
maintenance?

b   What attitude did the City Council take towards the royalist
occupation?

* * *c*   Explain and comment on (i) 'the Queenes comminge to Towne' (lines

15 and 16) (ii) 'Overseers of the Comon' (lines 40 and 41)
(iii) 'Scavenger' (line 42) (iv) 'prince Maurice' (line 46).

* *d* Examine lines 57 and 58 and compare them with the content of
document 5. Why had the people of Bath become so disillusioned
with the war?

5 Local Distress

We the Mayor, Aldermen, and Citizens of Bathe, in fear and trouble,
beseeche you to give advices to your son, touching our cities distress at
this present time, that he may in such wise get favour from the
commander to spare further levies, as we hear the troops are coming
5 onward for our city, and our houses are emptied of all useful furniture,
and much broken and disfigured; our poore suffer for want of victuals,
and rich we have none. God assist your love and friendship to us, and
favour your good will herein. Your son hathe good interest in the army,
and we doubt not will use his endeavours to succour and save his poore
10 neighbours. Warrants are come to raise horse, but we have none left;
Colonel Sandford doth promise his assistance, as much as he is able. We
have now 400 in the town and many more coming; God protect us from
pillage. We remain
Your sincere welwishers to command.
15 Bathe City, Feb. 1646.
        Letter to John Harington, Esq. of Kelston

Good Sir,
It is commanded me to give the thanks of our Cittie of Bath, and all its
inhabitants, to you for your good care and concern in providing your
20 owne company to come hither, and thereby preventing such disorder as
doth often happen, too oft, under soldier-like quarterings. The troop
behaved well, as it was expected your good direction did so endeavour
they should. Major Hewlet got in the levies as commanded, in such
manner as the rate observed all over the west. Many citizens had no
25 monies ready, and were threatened with pillage. Eighteen horses were
provided at the market house, and delivered up, as you desired; but the
men required were excused on your desiring, nor was any seizure made,
or plunder, except in liquors and bedding. The town-house was filled
with troops that came from Marlborow in their march westward. I have
30 sent out 5 men and 3 horses, but have no orders for more yet. God
preserve our Kingdom from these sad troubles much longer! . . .
    Our meal was taken by the Marlborow troop, but they restored it
again to many of the poorer sort. Our beds they occupied entirely, but no
greater mischief has happened as yet . . . . We have no divine service as
35 yet; the Churches are full of the troops, furniture and bedding. Pardon
my haste, as I have sent this by a poor man who may suffer if he is found
out, and I dare not send a man on purpose on horseback, as the horse

would be taken. We all commend our love and duties to you, from

Your true friend,

40 Robert Jones, sen.

Letter to Captain Harington, *Nugae Antiquae*, 1779, Vol 2, pp 278–87

Questions

a What particular demands did an approaching army feel entitled to make on local inhabitants?

b In what practical ways was Captain Harington able to assist the citizens of Bath following their request?

c How had the everyday life of ordinary people around Bath been affected by the Civil War?

* d Bath and its corporation were largely parliamentarian in political outlook. In what way do these letters lend support to the views of A. M. Everitt (see document 1)? In what way do they weaken his argument?

* e Compare these letters with the report of John Ashe in document 2. What main differences in the attitude of the local people are evident? How do you account for such a change?

6 Local Solidarity

. . . Bath Corporation reflected these tensions. Although the City Council was largely parliamentarian in its sympathies, although it continued to return puritan M.P.s like Popham, Ashe and Prynne to Westminster, it nevertheless contained an active group of royalists . . . .
5 The members of this group continued to sit side by side with the parliamentarians no matter which army was in actual control of the city. They were, after all, close neighbours and friends. Like them, they were concerned that the daily life of the city should not be too greatly disrupted by the national crisis. Like them, they were mainly drawn from the
10 wealthier class of traders, craftsmen and inkeepers who were interested in maintaining the flow of business . . . . Although they begged to differ over national issues, they were equally anxious to work together on local matters of common concern.

When the war ended, there seemed to be even more reason for
15 continuing this close relationship. Certainly the debates recorded in the *Council Minute Books* give no indication of any intention to remove the royalists from their midst – not at least until 27th September, 1647. On that day the Corporation decided quite suddenly by a majority of 18 votes to 10 'that Sergent Hyde shall be removed from his place and a new
20 Recorder chosen'. The important office of Recorder had been held for several years by Robert Hyde, a member of the notorious royalist family. During the war Robert had served in person with Prince Rupert. Even

so, the Corporation's action had been taken only after Parliament had
passed an Ordinance on 9th September requesting the removal of
25 royalists from local government. Most of the local councillors were more
than happy to forgive and forget — a fact vividly illustrated when, three
weeks later, they agreed to quash their original decision and agreed 'that
there shall be no election for a new Recorder, but the Sergt. Hyde shall
stand'.
30   The Commons, however, thought otherwise. On 4th October, they
therefore passed a more precise and forceful Ordinance, which put
irresistible pressure on local authorities:

> Be it declared, ordered and ordained by the Lords and Commons in Parliament
> assembled That no person whatsoever that hath been in arms against the
35 Parliament, or hath been aiding or assisting the forces of the enemy, or hath
> been or is sequestered, shall be elected, constituted Mayor, Alderman, Bailiff,
> Sheriff, Justice of the Peace, Steward of any Court, Constable, or any other
> officer. . . . And in case any such persons as aforesaid be elected into any of the
> Offices aforesaid . . . the Lords and Commons do declare all such elections to
40 be void and null.

Faced with this ultimatum, Bath Corporation had little choice. On 13th
December, 1647 they agreed to expel the royalist group *en bloc*. Samuel
Wintle, Philip Sherwood, Henry Chapman, Robert Sheppard, Robert
Fisher, Robert Hyde and Thomas Gibbs all relinquished their places. The
45 first four of these were actually present when the decision was taken.
William Prynne was then elected as the new Recorder, gaining eighteen
votes against the four received by the other candidate, John Harington. It
is worth recording, however, that Robert Fisher was re-instated in 1651
and that, shortly after the Restoration in 1660, Robert Sheppard, Henry
50 Chapman, Samuel Wintle and Robert Hyde were all back in their former
positions.
    John Wroughton, *The Civil War in Bath and North Somerset*,
    1973, pp 33–4, 112–13

Questions

a   Explain in your own words why parliamentarians and royalists had
    tolerated each other's presence on the City Council during the Civil
    War.

* b   Why was parliament in London anxious to remove all known
    royalists from local government office after the war ended?

* c   What evidence is there both here and in the previous documents to
    suggest 'a conflict between loyalty to the nation and loyalty to the
    county community' (See document 1, lines 30 and 31)?

* d   Explain briefly (i) 'a member of the notorious royalist family' (line 21)
    (ii) 'sequestered' (line 36) (iii) 'office of Recorder' (line 20).

* e   In what way can a local study of the Civil War deepen and modify our
    understanding of the national conflict?

VI The Execution of Charles I

Introduction

When the Second Civil War ended, the frustrations and bitterness which had steadily been mounting against the king's duplicity finally reached fever pitch. Many petitions were dispatched to London from various parts of the country demanding 'impartial justice' for *all* those involved in causing the recent bloodshed. This feeling was particularly strong in the army where Republicans and Levellers were extremely active. After much debate the council of army officers meeting at St Albans (18 November 1648) finally agreed to send a 'Remonstrance' to parliament. Largely the work of Henry Ireton, it demanded the trial of the king and the reform of the constitution. Cromwell, on duty with his regiment in Yorkshire, was informed of the decision.

Meanwhile, parliament itself, dominated by Denzil Holles and the presbyterian 'peace party', had resolved to re-open negotiations with the king. In the so-called Newport treaty, resulting from lengthy discussions on the Isle of Wight, Charles accepted that all military forces should be controlled by parliament for at least twenty years. With this security achieved, they rejected the army's 'Remonstrance' in favour of extending the Newport negotiations. The army's reaction was immediate and decisive. A 'purge' of the Commons by Colonel Pride and other officers ended with forty-five members being arrested and 186 being secluded.

With the removal of this 'peace party', the remnant (or 'Rump') voted to end negotiations with the king and to establish a high court of justice which would bring him to trial (1 January 1649). This proved to be difficult. Most lawyers refused to associate themselves with what was clearly an illegal court. Eventually 135 men were nominated to take part, though most agreed only under extreme pressure. Average attendances at sessions seldom amounted to more than seventy. Only fifty-nine finally signed the death warrant. This atmosphere of tension and fear was best illustrated by the president of the court (John Bradshaw) who wore a bullet-proof helmet under his normal felt hat. Throughout the trial Charles refused to recognise the court, refused to plead to the charge and refused to defend himself. He died with considerable dignity. Within a few days the prince of Wales, then in Holland, had assumed the title of King Charles II.

Further Reading

F. M. G. Higham, *Charles I, a study* (London, 1932)

J. G. Muddiman (ed.), *Trial of King Charles the First* (Edinburgh and London, 1928)

C. V. Wedgwood, *The Trial of Charles I* (Collins, 1964)

1   The Judgement of the Court

Whereas the Commons of England assembled in Parliament, have by their late Act . . . authorised and constituted us an High Court of Justice for the trying and judging of the said Charles Stuart for the crimes and treasons in the said Act mentioned . . . in pursuance of the said Act, a
5 charge of high treason and other high crimes was, in the behalf of the people of England, exhibited against him, and read openly unto him, wherein he was charged, that he, the said Charles Stuart, being admitted King of England, and therein trusted with a limited power to govern by, and according to the law of the land and not otherwise; and by his trust,
10 oath, and office, being obliged to use the power committed to him for the good and benefit of the people, and for the preservation of their rights and liberties; yet, nevertheless, out of a wicked design to erect and uphold in himself an unlimited and tyrannical power to rule according to his will, and to overthrow the rights and liberties of the people, and to take away
15 and make void the foundations thereof, and of all redress and remedy of misgovernment, which by the fundamental constitutions of this Kingdom were reserved on the people's behalf in the right and power of frequent and successive Parliaments; he, the said Charles Stuart . . . hath traitorously and maliciously levied war against the present Parliament,
20 and people therein represented . . . . This Court is fully satisfied in their judgments and consciences, that he has been and is guilty of the wicked design and endeavours in the said charge set forth; . . . and that he hath been and is the occasioner, author, and continuer of the said unnatural, cruel, and bloody wars, and therein guilty of high treason, and of the
25 murders, rapines, burnings, spoils, desolations, damage, and mischief to this nation acted and committed in the said war, and occasioned thereby. For all which treasons and crimes this Court doth adjudge that he, the said Charles Stuart, as a tyrant, traitor, murderer, and public enemy to the good people of this nation, shall be put to death by the severing of his
30 head from his body.

Sentence of the High Court of Justice, 27 January 1649

Questions

a   What, according to the court, were the traditional limitations and obligations placed upon the power of the king (lines 8–12)?

b Why were 'frequent and successive Parliaments' so important to the people (line 18)?

c Explain, why the court found Charles 'guilty of high treason' (line 24).

* d What was unusual about the composition of (i) 'the Commons of England assembled in Parliament' and (ii) the 'High Court of Justice' at the date of this document (lines 1–2)?

* e Explain how the 'rights and liberties of the people' (line 14) had been undermined in the reign of Charles 1.

* f Outline the circumstances which caused the Court to declare that Charles had 'levied war against the present Parliament' (line 19).

2 The Judgement of a Regicide

In January 1648/9, the court sat, the King was brought to his trial. . . . One thing was remarked in him by many of the court, that when the blood spilt in many of the battles where he was in his own person, and had caused it to be shed by his own command, was laid to his
5   charge, he heard it with disdainful smiles, and looks and gestures which rather expressed sorrow that all the opposite party to him were not cut off, than that any were: and he stuck not to declare in words, that no man's blood spilt in this quarrel troubled him except one, meaning the Earl of Strafford. The gentlemen that were appointed his judges, and
10 divers others, saw in him a disposition so bent on the ruin of all that opposed him, and of all the righteous and just things they had contended for, that it was upon the consciences of many of them, that if they did not execute justice upon him, God would require at their hands all the blood and desolation which should ensue by their suffering him to escape, when
15 God had brought him into their hands. Although the malice of the malignant party and their apostate brethren seemed to threaten them, yet they thought they ought to cast themselves upon God, while they acted with a good conscience for him and for their country. Some of them afterwards, for excuse, belied themselves, and said they were under the
20 awe of the army, and overpersuaded by Cromwell and the like; but it is certain that all men herein were left to their free liberty of acting, neither persuaded nor compelled . . . . As for Mr Hutchinson, although he was very much confirmed in his judgment concerning the cause, yet herein being called to an extraordinary action, whereof many were of several
25 minds, he addressed himself to God by prayer; . . . and finding no check, but a confirmation in his conscience that it was his duty to act as he did, he, upon serious debate, both privately and in his addresses to God, and in conferences with conscientious, upright, unbiased persons, proceeded to sign the sentence against the King . . . and therefore he cast himself upon
30 God's protection.

Lucy Hutchinson, *Memoirs of the Life of Colonel Hutchinson*, 1846, pp 334–6

Questions

* *a* Who were 'the gentlemen that were appointed his judges' (line 9)? What 'righteous and just things' (line 11) did they feel would be ruined by Charles 1?

  b Which parts of this extract appear to be based more on bias than on historical fact?

  c Which aspects of puritan belief does this passage illustrate?

* *d* Explain the historical background to the remark 'that no man's blood spilt in this quarrel troubled him except one, meaning the Earl of Strafford' (lines 7—9).

3 The Judgement of the King

About ten in the morning the King was brought from St. James's, walking on foot through the Park, with a regiment of foot, part before and part behind him, with colours flying, drums beating . . . up the stairs into the gallery and so into the Cabinet Chamber . . . where he
5 continued at his devotion, refusing to dine; only about an hour before he came forth he drank a glass of claret wine, and eat a peace of bread about twelve at noon . . . . The scaffold was hung round with black, and the floor covered with black, and the Axe and Block hid in the middle of the Scaffold. There were divers Companies of Foot, and Troops of Horse
10 placed on the one side of the scaffold towards Charing Cross, and the multitudes of people that came to be spectators, very great. The King being come upon the scaffold, look'd very earnestly on the Block, and asked Col. Hacker if there were no higher; and then spake thus (directing his speech chiefly to Colonel Tomlinson) . . . .
15   All the world knows that I never did begin a war with the two Houses of Parliament . . . for I do believe that ill instruments between them and me has been the chief cause of all this bloodshed . . . . I have forgiven all the world, and even those in particular that have been the chief causers of my death . . . . For the people; And truly I desire their liberty and
20 freedom as much as anybody whomsoever, but I must tell you, that their liberty and freedom consists in having of government; those laws by which their life and their goods may be most their own. It is not for having share in government that is pertaining to them; A subject and a sovereign are clean different things, and therefore until you do put the
25 people in that liberty as I say, certainly they will never enjoy themselves. Sir, it was for this that I am come here. If I would have given way to an arbitrary way, for to have all laws changed according to the power of the Sword, I needed not to have come here, and therefore I tell you . . . that I am the martyr of the people . . . . Then the King turning to Dr Juxon
30 said, I have a good cause and a gracious God on my side.

    King Charles his Speech made upon the Scaffold at Whitehall-Gate

Questions

a What personal qualities of Charles I are revealed by this extract?
* b Compare this extract with extracts 1 and 2. How does the king's view
     on the following matters differ from those expressed by the court and
     by Mrs Hutchinson (i) responsibility for the Civil War (ii) the
     liberty of the people (iii) kingship (iv) the will of God?

4 The Judgement of a Bystander

At the later end of the year 1648 I had leave given me to go to London to
see my father, and during my stay there at that time at Whitehall it was
that I saw the beheading of King Charles the First. He went by our door
on foot each day that he was carried by water to Westminster, for he took
5 barge at Gardenstayres where we lived, and once he spake to my father
and said: Art thou alive yet! On the day of his execution, which was
Tuesday, Jan. 30th, I stood amongst the crowd in the street before
Whitehall gate, where the scaffold was erected, and saw what was done,
but was not so near as to hear anything. The blow I saw given, and can
10 truly say with a sad heart; at the instant whereof, I remember well, there
was such a groan by the thousands then present, as I never heard before
and desire I may never hear again. There was according to order one
Troop immediately marching from-wards Charing Cross to
Westminster and another from-wards Westminster to Charing Cross
15 purposely to masker the people, and to disperse and scatter them, so that I
had much ado amongst the rest to escape home without hurt.
     Diaries and Letters of Philip Henry, ed. M. H. Lee, 1882

Questions

a What internal evidence is there in this extract to suggest that it is not
   entirely an impartial account?
* b What details given in this account of the execution are confirmed by
     those in extract 3?
c In what way does this represent a valuable piece of historical evidence?

5 The Judgement of a Foreign Observer

The poor King of England has at last lost both crown and life by the hand
of the executioner, like a common criminal, in London, before all the
people, without anyone speaking in his favour and by the judicial
sentence of his own subjects. The accompanying narrative gives the
5 particulars. History affords no example of the like. It is a shame to all
contemporary sovereigns, who for the sake of revenge against each other

about trifles have allowed themselves to be confronted by so imposing a spectacle, of the worst possible example.

The Prince of Wales, at the Hague, immediately assumed the royal title, although the Kingdom has pronounced him ineligible, and denounces as guilty of treason anyone who calls himself King of England. The States sent their condolences by a deputy from each province. In reply the King merely said that his sole comfort amid so many disasters was to find himself among them, through whose help he looked for his restoration, under God. They at once recalled the Ambassador Pauw, and some wished to recall the ordinary Joachimi as well, so as not to give any sanction to their proceedings, but on second thoughts, as the ambassadors of Spain, France, Portugal and others remain, they have ordered Joachimi to do the same, especially as the Commonwealth, as the English government now styles itself, has informed the States that all their merchants and goods will be treated over there like the native English, and that they mean to form a government resembling that of the Provinces in every respect, both ecclesiastical and civil, a thing easier said than done.

The States were to compliment the new King on his accession, but they are not yet agreed among themselves what to call him. Meanwhile he is drawing up letters to acquaint all the powers of Europe with the tragedy, and to ask for help . . . . All commiserate his misfortune and his innocence, although those who unite to avenge it may be few in number.

The Venetian Ambassador at Munster to the Doge and Senate

Questions

a What motives did the United Provinces apparently have in changing their minds about the recall of Joachimi (line 16)?

* b Explain why the Venetian Ambassador felt that the execution was 'a shame to all contemporary sovereigns' (lines 5 and 6) and why he referred to it as 'the worst possible example' (line 8).

* c How correct was the judgement in the last sentence? Was *any* help given to the prince?

* d State briefly the relationship between the new Commonwealth and (i) Spain (ii) France (iii) Portugal in the years 1649–53.

* e Did the new Commonwealth maintain its promise to the United Provinces 'that all their merchants and goods will be treated over there like the native English' (lines 20–21) in the years 1649–53?

6   The Judgement of a Modern Historian

The Trial of Charles I is one of the most startling – perhaps the most startling – event of English history. It certainly astounded all Europe in 1649. 'The most horrible and detestable parricide ever committed by Christians – in words such as these it was almost everywhere condemned. Only in some of the Swiss Protestant cantons does there seem to have been a favourable reception to the event.

Kings had been deposed and killed before. But this was the first time that a King had been arraigned under his title as King and in the name of his people. Three weeks before putting him on trial the House of Commons proclaimed that 'The people under God are the source of all just power'. They went on to the rather less convincing proposition that the remnant of the House of Commons elected eight years previously truly represented the people. The charge was drawn up against 'Charles Stuart, King of England' with the emphasis on his royal office. At the trial itself, the chief prosecuting Counsel asserted in Westminister Hall that he was acting 'on behalf of my clients the People of England'.

There was a fanatic resolution in the minds of the leaders (if not always in the minds of the secondary actors in this event) to show that no divinity hedged the position of a King, that he was nothing more than the highest officer of State, a steward appointed by and for people, who could be called to account by them. 'We will cut off his head with the Crown on it', Cromwell is alleged to have said. 'With the Crown on it' – this was the novelty of the business. That a monarch should come to grief through deposition, should be deprived of his royal office and his sacred character, and subsequently done to death – that had happened a number of times. Edward II, Richard II, Henry VI and Mary Stuart had all died violent deaths only after deposition.

But Charles was tried and executed as King and his death was intended as an attack on the mystique of Kingship itself. This was new in 1649. It was the work of a dominant group of officers in the Parliamentary Army led by Oliver Cromwell the Lieutenant-General and his son-in-law Henry Ireton, seconded by such political Republicans as Colonel Edmund Ludlow and such religious fanatics as Colonel Thomas Harrison. They acted in conjunction with a small resolute republican group in the House of Commons, the Commonwealth men as they were called, of whom Harry Marten was the most significant . . . .

The King for his part was no less fanatical. He believed with immovable constancy that God had given him paramount authority over his subjects, to protect them and their liberties, but as *he* saw them not as *they* saw them. He could not, therefore, abandon his power or agree to its limitation without committing a sin against the ordinance of God. He could not recognise the so-called authority of the people, still less of the unprecedented Court set up to try him, because to do so would have been not only politically but morally wrong. Thus his trial presented, in its most dramatic form, a confrontation between two irreconcilable theories of government . . . .

The war solved nothing, because parliament had assumed that when the King was defeated he would bow to the logic of defeat and accept their terms; but he could not do so. Defeated, he still refused their terms. He evaded the issue; he tried to play off the Scots against the English, parliament against the army; finally he engineered a new Royalist rising coupled with an invasion from Scotland – the events known as the Second Civil War. It is beside the point to accuse Charles of dishonesty in his dealings. Believing as he did, he was morally compelled to do all in his power to regain his authority. Any means he could find to outwit his opponents was therefore acceptable to him. But if he for his part was driven to extremes by his theory of Kingship and his faith in it, they were driven to what they did by the sheer necessity of the political impasse in which they found themselves. As Cromwell put it, 'Providence and necessity' compelled them to exact a final reckoning from the King, because there was no other way of restoring peace and stability to England. The Second Civil War of 1648 made the King's death inevitable . . . .

Inevitably in any account of his trial the King appears in a more sympathetic light than his accusers. He was one and they were many. But politically, in the long run, the greater courage was theirs. Convinced, in the words of Cromwell, that God had witnessed against the King and that he deserved death, they chose to defy convention; they did not engineer some hole-in-the-corner murder; they sought (however unsuccessfully) to demonstrate the guilt of the Monarch in the traditional seat of English justice, in Westminster Hall, before a full audience of his subjects, in a trial that was fully reported. As one of their supporters proudly predicted a few days after the King's death, their actions would 'live and remain upon record to the perpetual honour of the English state, who took no dark and doubtful way, no indirect by-course, but went in the open and plain path of Justice, Reason, Law and Religion'. John Milton, in yet more eloquent terms, praised the glory of the act, 'God has inspired the English to be the first of mankind who have not hesitated to judge and condemn their King.'

> C. V. Wedgwood, 'The Trial of Charles I' in R. H. Parry (ed.)
> *The English Civil War and After*, 1970, pp 41–3, 56

Questions

a What was so unusual about the trial and execution of Charles I?

b Explain why the two theories of Government were 'irreconcilable' (line 45).

* *c* From your knowledge of the period, show how Charles I 'tried to play off the Scots against the English, parliament against the army' (lines 50 and 51).

d Why did the Second Civil War make the king's death 'inevitable' (line 63)?

e What qualities does Wedgwood see in the regicides?

* *f* What main contribution to this period were made by (i) Ireton (line 32) (ii) Ludlow (line 33) (iii) Harrison (line 34) (iv) Marten (line 36) (v) Milton (line 76)?

VII The Parliaments of Commonwealth and Protectorate

Introduction

In December 1648, the council of army officers ordered Colonel Pride to 'purge' the Long Parliament of those members who were obstructing the army in its desire to bring Charles I to trial. About 186 members in all were 'secluded' or prevented from taking their seats in the Commons. A further forty-five were sent to prison. Out of a total of 471 MPs, only about seventy-one continued along the road which was to bring the king to the scaffold. But who *were* the revolutionaries? How did they differ as people from those who were excluded? Was it simply a question of Independents versus Presbyterians?

In attempting to answer these questions, David Underdown has continued the recent trend away from a total emphasis on social and economic aspects of the Great Rebellion. Interest in political issues has partly been re-awakened by the introduction of new statistical and analytical techniques. In 1954 two books set the pattern – Douglas Brunton and Donald Pennington's *Members of the Long Parliament*, and Mary Keeler's *The Long Parliament 1640–1641, A Biographical Study of its Members*. These, together with Underdown's *Pride's Purge* and Blair Worden's *The Rump Parliament*, have given a detailed study of the complexity of party groupings within the Commons.

Blair Worden, as a result of his research, challenged the long-established theory that the Rump acted throughout in mere self-interest. Why, therefore, did they attempt to hold new elections in 1653 with such 'preposterous haste' – and why did Cromwell object when he had previously been so much in favour? Views of historians are frequently being challenged and modified as new facts come to light and new techiques are perfected. Ultimate truth is difficult to achieve. Or, as Underdown admits – 'The statistics have spoken. They have not worked miracles; they have not answered unanswerable questions.'

Further Reading

Christopher Hill, *Puritanism and Revolution* (Secker & Warburg, 1958; Panther edn, 1968)

Ivan Roots, *The Great Rebellion, 1642–1660* (Batsford, 1966)

David Underdown, *Pride's Purge* (Oxford, 1971)

Blair Worden, *The Rump Parliament* (Cambridge, 1974)

1 Pride's Purge 1648. Underdown's Analysis of the Purgers and the Purged

The Revolution of 1648–9 was over. But what actually had happened? In a general way, of course, we already know. We know that Parliament was purged, roughly who was purged, by whom, and for what ostensible reasons. Nevertheless there are many questions that narrative history cannot answer, that are still worth asking of a historical situation such as Pride's Purge. Were there, for instance, significant differences between supporters and opponents of the revolution in such things as age, education, religion and social status? A sociologist would wish to answer these questions of a sample of the entire 'political nation'. We cannot do that, but we can at least make some effort to do so of the only large group at our diposal, the Members of Parliament. We need not expect that quantification will magically provide exact answers to all questions; history is not an exact science. The vexing difficulties of definition and classification, the imprecision, for example, of such terms as Presbyterian and Independent, help to undermine the most carefully compiled statistics. The evidence about individual M.P.s varies enormously in both quality and quantity . . . .

The 471 M.P.s (excluding vacancies, absentees etc.) can be divided into five groups: the active revolutionaries who openly committed themselves to the revolution while it was in progress during December and January; the conformists who avoided formal commitment at that time, but accepted the *fait accompli* in February, when they could no longer be incriminated in the execution of the King; the abstainers, who were not actually secluded, but showed their opposition by staying away from Parliament at least until the spring of 1649; the victims of the Purge who were secluded; and the hard core of the Army's enemies, who suffered imprisonment as well as seclusion . . . . Unfortunately the evidence on which the analysis must be based is distressingly imperfect. The Journals of the Commons tell us who were named to committees during the critical period, but only rarely (as when they made reports or acted as tellers) who were actually present. No political diaries record these passionate months, and very little private correspondence; letters are the first victims of revolution. Newspapers and pamphlets are uncertain guides, while the Whitelocks and Ludlows, in memoirs written years afterwards, speak only in general terms . . . .

At the end of this tedious methodological exercise, we have then 471 M.P.s divided into the following categories, which will for convenience in future by referred to by initials.

	Revolutionaries (R)	71 (15 %)
40	Conformists (C)	83 (18 %)
	Abstainers (A)	86 (18 %)
	Secluded (S)	186 (40 %)
	Imprisoned (I)	45 (9 %)

45 . . . The statistics have spoken. They have not worked miracles; they have not answered unanswerable questions. They have shown that there were indeed significant differences between the purgers and the purged in some respects, but in others only marginal ones. They have not shown that the revolution was *essentially* about either politics or religion; or that it was essentially either a class struggle or a mere *coup d'état* by a crowd of 50 backwoods outsiders trying to get in. They do perhaps suggest that it was a mixture of all these things.

. . . The typical R was a married man in his mid-forties. He had probably inherited an estate, but was quite possibly a younger son. He had gone to one of the Inns of Court, most likely Gray's Inn, and was less 55 likely to have attended a university. He may possibly have come from the north-east of England. He had no previous parliamentary experience, entered the Long Parliament in a by-election after August, 1645, and attached himself to the radical wing of the Independents; he joined the Speaker in seceding to the Army at the end of July 1647. In religion he 60 probably, but not necessarily, turned to Independency. Of county gentry status, he came of a rather insecure family, and was probably not a rich man, having a pre-war income of less than £500 a year; if richer he may well have been in serious debt. He was likely to have large financial claims against the State, and to recover some of these debts in the form of 65 Church, royalist or Crown lands, in that order of preference. He may have been an office-holder, and if not was quite likely to become one after the revolution . . . .

The typical S was a married man in his mid-forties, and had probably inherited an estate, though he might possibly be the heir to one with a 70 father still living. He had gone to Oxford or an Inn of Court, preferring Lincoln's Inn or Middle Temple before the others. He too came either from the south-east or the south-west. Another Recruiter without previous experience in Parliament, he may have been under suspicion of having flirted with the Royalists, and if he adopted a recognizable 75 political stance in the Long Parliament it was as a Presbyterian; he probably stayed at Westminster during the Speaker's absence in July and August 1647. His religious views were outwardly Presbyterian, though secretly he may have preferred moderate episcopacy. Of greater gentry status, stable family, and large income (over £1,000 a year), he had no 80 claims against the State, was therefore very unlikely to have bought or to be contemplating buying confiscated lands, and was not an office-holder.

He was in fact a very solid and representative country gentleman.

The typical I was older, nearly fifty, probably married, and with an inherited estate. He had been educated at both Oxford and an Inn, most likely Middle Temple, and came from either the south-east or the Midlands. A man of experience, he was an original member of the Long Parliament, who may well have sat in the Short Parliament and even in those of the 1620's. During the war he had been attached to either the peace party or the middle group, and was more probably Presbyterian (though still just possibly middle group) between 1645 and 1648. Even if not one of the Eleven Members or their immediate supporters, he had stayed at Westminster in July and August 1647. Like his S colleague, he was a Presbyterian in religion, perhaps at heart preferring moderate episcopacy. One of the country gentry, of possibly insecure family, he was nevertheless a rich man, with an income of over £1,000 a year. He was likely to have claims against the State, possibly large ones, but did not recover these debts in the form of confiscated lands. He may have been an office-holder in 1648, but if so probably lost his place after the Purge.

David Underdown, *Pride's Purge*, 1971, pp 208, 210–11, 220, 253–6

Questions

* *a* From Underdown's comments in the first paragraph on the nature of history, explain (i) what are the sort of questions, in general, 'that narrative history cannot answer' (lines 4 and 5) (ii) why 'history is not an exact science' (line 13).

b Why are (i) letters 'the first victims of revolution' (line 33) (ii) newspapers and pamphlets 'uncertain guides' (lines 33 and 34)?

c What were the main differences and similarities between the typical 'Revolutionary' and the typical 'Secluded', according to Underdown's analysis?

d What were the main differences and similarities between the typical 'Secluded' and the typical 'Imprisoned'?

e What are Underdown's general conclusions from the study? Is this type of research valuable?

* *f* Explain, from your knowledge of the period, what you understand by (i) 'he joined the Speaker in seceding to the Army at the end of July 1647' (lines 58 and 59) (ii) 'another Recruiter' (line 72) (iii) 'During the war he had been attached to either the peace party or the middle group' (lines 88 and 89) (iv) 'the Eleven Members' (line 91).

2 The Rump 1649–53 Worden's Analysis of its Dissolution

The conflict of 20 April 1653 was not between a parliament determined to

perpetuate its power and an army resolved to hold elections, but between
a parliament which had resolved to hold elections (of whatever kind) and
an army determined to prevent it from doing so. The dissolution was not
a victory for St. John and the advocates of open elections: it was the
triumph of Harrison and the prophets of the imminent millennium. At
some point before the dissolution, in other words, the roles of parliament
and army were reversed. Previously the army had pressed for a speedy
dissolution while the Rump had resisted it: now the Rump was arranging
elections while the army tried to stem the House's 'preposterous
haste . . . .'

Yet if the conviction and the passion with which the House proceeded
on 20 April were novel, its resolve to hold elections was much older. The
Rump had never regarded itself as anything other than an interim
government, and it had always acted on the assumption that it would
eventually make way for a newly elected parliament. In all its resolutions
on the subject of elections, from March 1649 onwards, it implicitly
acknowledged that by postponing them it was compromising between
the ideal and the necessity; elections were desirable, but they were not yet
practicable.

Before Worcester, this attitude had the support of the army officers.
After Worcester, the attitude was hardened by the army's hostility to the
Rump; the demand for a speedy dissolution met with resentment and
obstruction, and attempts were made, in May 1652 and early 1653, to
revive the recruiting plan. Yet Cromwell's assertion on the evening
before the dissolution that fresh elections were undesirable until the
electorate should 'forget monarchy' reminds us, as does John Jones's
warning in the autumn of 1651, that there were eminently sensible
reasons for postponing fresh elections and for contemplating recruiter
ones. That historians automatically attribute to mere selfishness the
Rump's prolonged reluctance to dissolve is due entirely to the imbalance
in the surviving evidence. The plausible explanation of the Rump's
behaviour after Worcester is that it intended to delay elections until the
army had been disbanded or at least reduced to impotence, and until, in
Jones's words, 'burdens' had been 'taken off' and the Commonwealth
given 'some time to take root in the interests of men.' The way would
thus have been cleared for the civilian, constitutional settlement for which
the Rump had always striven. In January 1653, however, it at last became
clear that the Rump would be obliged to dissolve before the army
were disbanded. Faced with this realisation the House changed not its
heart, but its strategy. The recruiting scheme, never seen as more than an
interim solution, was finally abandoned, and the decision to proceed with
the bill for a new representative taken. That decision, although initially
welcomed by the army, was of course not in the army's interests. For by
resolving to hold elections before the Commonwealth had 'taken root in
the affections of men,' the rumpers were jeopardising the
Commonwealth's survival. That they were prepared to do so is a
reminder of their continuing lack of commitment to the form of

government which had emerged after the execution of the King. There is no doubt that the bill would have led to the election of members who had not sat since December 1648 and of men of similar views. What the Rump was plotting on 20 April was not the perpetuation of its authority; it was revenge for Pride's Purge . . . .

No doubt many rumpers enjoyed the experience of power and developed a taste for it, but there is no reason to suppose that they believed they had an exclusive right to it. Their decision in April 1653 to pass a bill from which, as individuals, they had nothing to gain and everything to lose suggests the opposite. Before Worcester, the Rump had served its purpose: the royalists had been defeated; army radicalism had been contained; the threat of social revolution had been averted; constitutional forms had been preserved. The country, if not governed in the way either rumpers or soldiers would have liked, had at least continued to be governed. After Worcester, however, the Rump had to concern itself not only with its own short-term survival but with long-term problems of political settlement; and the fracture of the coalition between parliament and army, the increasing stagnation and bitterness of politics, and the hardening of both presbyterian and radical opinion in the country made it plain that settlement could never be achieved so long as the Rump remained in power. Accordingly, in the words of the letter attributed to Marten, it was the rumpers' 'endeavour' that 'the settlement of these nations, which they saw themselves not able to accomplish, might be performed by others.' However radically rumpers had differed in the past, they had come by April, 1653 to agree with St. John that, 'as the distractions then were,' fresh elections were 'the best and justest way of healing them' . . . .

The dissolution of the Rump marked the capture of Cromwell by the chosen. Of course, that is not all it marked. Cromwell did not need Fifth Monarchist fanaticism to disenchant him with the Rump, whose failings had long distressed him; and the news on 20 April that his intimate friends Vane and St. John had betrayed him was no doubt the final blow. We need not suppose that Cromwell, throughout the crisis leading to the dissolution, was in the grip of a millenarian trance. The reforms for which he had pressed in the House had been limited ones, drafted by men as moderate as Matthew Hale, John Owen and John Dury, and supported in the House by such equally moderate figures as Gilbert Pickering, Charles Fleetwood and Thomas Westrow. To those who put reform before parliamentary supremacy, the Rump had failed disastrously; and there is no doubting the Rump's ability to offend moderate reformers – or, indeed, its capacity for sheer cussedness . . . .

In the traditional view of the Rump there is a hiatus. The rumpers, it has seemed, were energetically radical in 1649; yet by 1653 they had become intolerably oligarchical, dilatory and corrupt. Both the initial radicalism and the subsequent decadence of the regime have been exaggerated. The explanation of the Rump's demise lay less in any change in its character, which had been largely determined in infancy, than in the changing requirements Cromwell made of it. Cromwell, the destroyer of the Commonwealth regime, had also, more than anyone else, been its architect. The Rump was his conservative solution to the problems of 1648–9. Thereafter it never displayed the reforming idealism he demanded of it. The wonder is that he ever imagined that it would.

Blair Worden, *The Rump Parliament, 1648–1653*, 1974, pp 373–4, 376–8, 380, 384

Questions

a What were the 'eminently sensible reasons' (lines 28 and 29) which, according to Worden, caused the Rump to delay new elections?

b Explain why the Rump's decision in 1653 to hold new elections was 'not in the army's interests' (line 44).

c What were the Rump's (i) main achievements before the battle of Worcester (ii) main problems afterwards?

d What main reasons does Worden advance against the charge of the Rump's selfishness?

e For what reasons did Cromwell approve of the Rump's dissolution?

* f Explain, from your knowledge of the period, what you understand by (i) 'Harrison and the prophets of the imminent millennium' (line 6) (ii) 'his intimate friends Vane and St. John had betrayed him' (lines 79 and 80) (iii) 'the reforms for which he had pressed' (lines 82 and 83).

3   Oliver Cromwell and his Parliaments 1653–8

(a) *Trevor-Roper's View of Cromwell's Failure*

Oliver Cromwell and his parliaments – the theme is almost a tragicomedy. Cromwell was himself a Member of Parliament; he was the appointed general of the armies of Parliament; and the Victorians, in the greatest days of parliamentary government, set up his statue outside the rebuilt Houses of Parliament. But what were Cromwell's relations with Parliament? The Long Parliament, which appointed him, he first purged by force and then violently expelled from authority. His own Parliament, the Parliament of the Saints, which to a large extent was nominated by his government, was carried away by hysteria, rent by intrigue and dissolved, after six months, by an undignified act of suicide. Of the parliaments of the Protectorate, elected on a new franchise and within new limits determined by the government, the first was purged by force within a week and dissolved, by a trick hardly distinguishable from fraud, before its legal term; the second was purged by fraud at the beginning and, when that fraud was reversed, became at once unmanageable and was dissolved within a fortnight. On a superficial view Cromwell was as great an enemy of Parliament as ever Charles I or Archbishop Laud had been, the only difference being that, as an enemy, he was more successful: he scattered all his parliaments and died in his bed, while theirs deprived them of their power and brought them both ultimately to the block.

Nevertheless, between Cromwell and the Stuarts, in this matter, there was a more fundamental difference than this; for even if he could never control his parliaments in fact, Cromwell at least never rejected them in theory. This is not because he was deliberately consistent with his own parliamentary past. Cromwell was deliberately consistent in nothing. No political career is so full of undefended inconsistencies as his. But he was fundamentally and instinctively conservative, and he saw in Parliament part of the natural order of things . : . .

And what were the positive ideals of these outraged but largely unpolitical conservative gentry? Naturally, in the circumstances, they were not very constructive. These men looked back, not forward; back from the House of Stuart which had so insulted them to the House of Tudor of which their fathers had spoken; and in the reign of Elizabeth they discovered, or invented, a golden age: an age when the Court had been, as it seemed, in harmony with the country and the Crown with its parliaments; an age when a Protestant queen, governing parsimoniously at home and laying only tolerable burdens on 'her faithful Commons', had nevertheless made England glorious abroad — head of the Protestant interest throughout the world, victor over Spain in the Indies, protector of the Netherlands in Europe. Since 1603 that glorious position had been lost . . . . None of them dreamed, in 1640, of revolution, either in Church or in State. They were neither separatists nor republicans. What they wanted was a King who, unlike Charles I, but like the Queen Elizabeth of their imagination, would work the existing institutions in the good old sense . . . .

Under Oliver Cromwell something was missing in the mechanics of parliamentary government. It was not merely that useful drop of oil with which Queen Elizabeth had now and then so gracefully lubricated the machine. It was something far more essential . . . . The methods by which Queen Elizabeth so effectively controlled her parliaments of – for the most part – unpolitical gentry are now, thanks to the great work of Sir John Neale and Professor Notestein, well known. They consisted, first, in electoral and other patronage and, secondly, in certain procedural devices among which the essential were two: the presence in Parliament of a firm nucleus of experienced Privy Councillors, and royal control over the Speaker . . . .

Like his fellow-squires (and like those liberal historians who virtuously blame the Tudors for 'packing' their parliaments) Cromwell tended to regard all parliamentary management as a 'cabal', a wicked interference with the freedom of Parliament. Therefore he supplied none, and when other more politically minded men sought to fill the void, he intervened to crush such indecent organisation. In this way he thought he was securing 'free parliaments' – free, that is, from caucus-control. Having thus secured a 'free parliament', he expected it automatically, as a result

65 merely of good advice, good intentions and goodwill, to produce 'good laws', as in the reign of his heroine Queen Elizabeth. He did not realise that Queen Elizabeth's parliaments owed their effectiveness not to such 'freedom', nor to the personal worthiness of the parties, nor to the natural harmony between them, but to that ceaseless vigilance, intervention and

70 management by the Privy Council which worthy Puritan back-benchers regarded as a monstrous limitation of their freedom. No wonder Cromwell's parliaments were uniformly barren . . . .

Thus it is really misleading to speak of 'Cromwell and his parliaments' as we speak of 'Queen Elizabeth and her parliaments', for in that positive

75 sense Cromwell – to his misfortune – had no parliaments: he only faced, in a helpless, bewildered manner, a succession of parliaments which he failed either to pack, to control or to understand. There was the Parliament of Hesilrige and Scot, the Parliament of Squibb and Moyer, the Parliament of Birch, the Parliament of Broghill, and the Parliament

80 of Hesilrige once again; but there was never a Parliament of Oliver Cromwell. Ironically, the one English sovereign who had actually been a Member of Parliament proved himself, as a parliamentarian, the most incompetent of them all. He did so because he had not studied the necessary rules of the game. Hoping to imitate Queen Elizabeth, who, by

85 understanding those rules, had been able to play upon 'her faithful Commons' as upon a well-tuned instrument, he failed even more dismally than the Stuarts..The tragedy is that whereas they did not believe in the system, he did.

H. R. Trevor-Roper, 'Oliver Cromwell and his Parliaments' in *Religion, the Reformation and Social Change*, 1967, pp 345–6, 348–9, 352–5, 389–91

Questions

* a From your knowledge of the period explain what you understand by (i) 'first purged by force and then violently expelled from authority' (lines 6 and 7) (ii) 'dissolved, after six months, by an undignified act of suicide' (line 10) (iii) 'the second was purged by fraud' (line 14).
  b What characteristics does Trevor-Roper see in Oliver Cromwell?
  c What sort of king and what sort of parliament did Cromwell desire according to Trevor-Roper?
  d Why did Cromwell fail 'even more dismally than the Stuarts' (lines 86 and 87) with his parliament?
* e Write briefly on the historical importance of (i) Hesilrige and Scot (line 78) (ii) Broghill (line 79).

(b) Hill's Critique of Trevor-Roper's View

He argues that Cromwell, like James I and Laud, was unable to 'manage' Parliament or elections, and suggests that this was due to incompetence, to the back-bencher attitude typical of the Independent small gentry. Professor Trevor-Roper almost conveys the impression that a Cecil or a John Robinson could have established the Protectorate on a secure basis. This assumes that 'Parliamentary management' is an art which can be applied irrespective of political circumstances. The Duke of Newcastle could control Parliaments because, in the words of Sir Lewis Namier, 'the nation was at one in all fundamental matters, and whenever that happy but uninspiring condition was reached, Parliamentary contests lose reality and unavoidably change into a fierce though bloodless struggle for places'. Burghley, though with more difficulty, could control Parliament because in the last resort the opposition preferred the existing government to any possible alternative. Under James and Charles, and still more in the sixteen-fifties, the political nation was not 'at one in all fundamental matters'. It was rent by political disagreements which led to civil war. The Parliamentarians were in sufficient agreement for Pym to be able to manage those who remained at Westminster; after the war was won political disagreements re-appeared which led to purges of Parliament and to military dictatorship. The feelings of Ludlow and Prynne about Oliver Cromwell were different from those of a disappointed office-seeker about the Duke of Newcastle. Even if Oliver had 'studied the necessary rules of the game', his enemies were more interested in bringing about Kingdom of God upon earth than in playing cricket. The Protector failed to come to terms with his first Parliament, and managed to do so with his second, not because Broghill was a better Parliamentary manager than Thurloe, still less because this opportunist ex-Royalist was seeking 'to save the real aims of the revolution', but because in 1656 the government was prepared to surrender to the political programme demanded by the majority in Parliament, whereas in 1654 it had not been. Without a change of policy by the executive, no amount of management could have secured it a majority, even with many M.P.s excluded. At such a price James I could have secured a favourable majority too: Buckingham did in 1624. 'Management' enables good Parliamentarians to obtain collaboration in working for agreed objectives, or in sharing out spoils when objectives are not in dispute; it does not enable the best politicians in the world to square circles.

Christopher Hill, 'Recent Interpretations of the Civil War' in *Puritanism and Revolution*, 1968, pp 22–4

Questions

a   Why does Hill feel that Trevor-Roper's charge of incompetence against Oliver Cromwell is unfair?

*   b   Why were 'the feelings of Ludlow and Prynne about Oliver Cromwell' different 'from those of a disappointed office-seeker about the Duke of Newcastle' (lines 20–22)?

*   c   In what way was the government in 1656 'prepared to surrender to the political programme demanded by the majority in Parliament' (lines 29 and 30)?

VIII   The Restoration 1660

Introduction

After the death of Oliver Cromwell in September 1658, his son Richard failed to display the qualities necessary to maintain the office of Protector. Army officers were quick to intervene. The Protectorate collapsed and the Rump was recalled amid mounting confusion. To restore order and prevent total anarchy, General Monck marched his army on London. There he insisted that the presbyterian members, excluded in Pride's Purge (1648), should be re-admitted to parliament. Charles II was now only a short step away from the throne. Acting on statesmanlike advice from Sir Edward Hyde and others, he issued an appealing declaration from Breda aimed at re-assuring his future subjects. Elections to a new 'Convention Parliament' returned a large majority favourable to a Restoration. The monarchy was re-established – but it was clearly not the monarchy of the 1630s. There was no Court of High Commission, no Star Chamber and certainly no right to raise taxation without parliament's consent. Charles tried hard to use his considerable personal charm to heal the various wounds which still festered. The first 'cavalier' parliament of the reign, however, proved itself far less tolerant. The so-called Clarendon Code (composed of the Corporation Act, the Uniformity Act, the Conventicle Act and the Five Mile Act) put effective shackles on presbyterian influence.

This brief background to events fails, of course, to answer the vital questions which need to be discussed. Why *did* the Protectorate collapse so quickly? Who really were the people behind the Restoration? Clearly they were not the cavaliers themselves. How far did Charles honour his promises made at Breda? Who were the victims of the Restoration?

Further Reading

Maurice Ashley, *Charles II* (Praeger, New York, 1971)
Godfrey Davies, *The Restoration of Charles II, 1658–1660* (Oxford, 1955)
David Ogg, *England in the Reign of Charles II* (Oxford, 1934)

1 Collapse of the Protectorate

How long before the Restoration began the great surge of enthusiasm which welcomed Charles II home to England? From the pages of Pepys and Clarendon and many a lesser witness, its warmth still glows across three hundred years. Was it the release of a national devotion to
5 monarchy and the Stuarts which only force had repressed during the long years of Puritan rule? So all Royalists assumed, and up to a point rightly; a plebiscite would probably have declared for the King at any time after the Civil War. But sentiment is one thing; a passion strong enough to unite men in effective action is rarer, and in this case only arose during that final
10 autumn and winter when the quarrelling heirs of the Long Parliament forfeited the very capacity to govern. It was a response to anarchy; the King returned only when the revolution had collapsed from within.

To this process the professed Royalists contributed very little. The strength of the King's cause was not to be measured in loyal toasts drunk
15 in private or vague offers of future service, and Royalist enterprises against the Commonwealth and Protectorate tell a sad story of divisions, jealousies, broken promises, baseless expectations of popular support, and a steadily growing wariness among the Old Cavaliers. As for the many others who washed their hands of regicide or grumbled at taxes and
20 redcoats, few were ready to face the cost, in violence and disorder, of exchanging Cromwell's rule for the King's. So long as government kept the peace and protected property, nothing could be so bad as a renewal of civil war.

Cromwell's death gave only short-lived encouragement to the King's
25 friends; Richard's quiet accession was nowhere questioned and widely welcomed . . . . Even the Royalists, the French ambassador reported, were glad to persuade themselves that honour no longer demanded their resistance. Richard's rule appealed to men of substance because it eschewed fanatical extremes in Church and state, and emphasized the
30 conservative trends of his father's later years. Moderation, however, was not enough. He brought to his task sincerity, a good presence, blameless morals, and the qualities of an easy-going, likeable country squire. But the precarious balance of interests left at Oliver's death called for constant, positive direction at the centre, and neither Richard nor the second-rate
35 men of his Privy Council could provide it. In the Parliament which met in January 1659 he could have commanded the support of a considerable majority, yet for lack of governmental leadership and management in the house the republican politicians who had disrupted Oliver's two parliaments were allowed to 'addle' this one too.

40 Richard's gravest weakness was his lack of standing in the army. The officers scarcely knew him, but they felt they had a much stronger claim to guide Oliver's successor than the conservative civilians whom he obviously preferred . . . . The Protectorate was falling before a 'confederated Triumvirate of republicans, sectaries and soldiers'. The end
45 came on April 21st, when Fleetwood summoned the regiments about

London to St. James's and Richard ordered a counter-rendezvous at Whitehall. Richard, deserted by all but a handful of troops, was forced to dissolve Parliament.

50 The generals had hoped to maintain a puppet Protectorate, but republican propaganda had convinced most of their subordinates that they could only recover God's favour for their cause by putting the clock back to a time before their fall from grace; they must restore the Commonwealth as it had been before Cromwell violated it. They had their way. On May 7th the little remnant of the Long Parliament, soon
55 known everywhere as the Rump, took up the reins of government as though six years' eclipse had been a month's adjournment.

A. H. Woolrych, *The Collapse of the Great Rebellion* (in *History Today*, September 1958, pp 606–7)

Questions

a   Why, according to Woolrych, did the Restoration not occur before 1660 despite a general sympathy towards monarchy?

b   Why did Richard Cromwell's accession fail at first to revive the hopes of royalist exiles?

c   What personal weaknesses helped to bring about Richard's fall?

* d   Explain what you understand by (i) 'the precarious balance of interests left at Oliver's death' (line 33) (ii) 'the republican politicians who had disrupted Oliver's two parliaments' (lines 38 and 39) (iii) 'they must restore the Commonwealth as it had been before Cromwell violated it' (lines 52 and 53).

2   Support for the Restoration

. . . By the end of 1659 shops could no longer be opened with safety. The law courts ceased to function. The Army had to live by free quarter, and it was but a small step from this to unrestricted plunder. In 1659–60, the censorship being once again unenforceable, pamphlets were published
5 calling for law reform, stable copyholds, and other Leveller objectives.

The Reverend Henry Newcombe supported the Restoration, but was ejected from his living as a Presbyterian in 1662. Later he looked back and asked himself whether it had been worth it. He decided it had. 'Though soon after the settlement of the nation we saw ourselves the despised and
10 cheated party, . . . yet, in all this I have suffered since, I look upon it as less than my trouble was from my fears then . . . .' So the Presbyterians sacrificed religion to social order. In April 1660 Milton had warned of the danger that religion and liberty would be prostituted to 'the vain and groundless apprehension that nothing but Kingship can restore
15 trade' . . . .

The decisive moment was the day in February 1660 when the militia was taken from the command of 'persons of no degree or quality' and

restored to 'the government of the nobility and principal gentry'. Pepys
stated the alternatives precisely in his *Diary* for 18th April 1660: 'Either
the fanatics must now be undone or the gentry and citizens throughout
England, and clergy, must fall, inspite of their militia and army.' The
gentry and citizens, the free, were opposed by the fanatics, the
republicans, the many-headed monster. Fear of the latter led the free to
look to Charles Stuart, 'out of love to themselves, not to him', Ralph
Joscelyn noted in his Diary . . . .

Popular rejoicing at the Restoration should not deceive us. Men of
property were pleased to feel that law, order and social stability, liberty
and property, were being restored with the King, discipline with the
Bishops. They brought rumps for the populace to roast, just as in 1623
they had paid for rejoicings at the return of Prince Charles from Spain.
But as Cromwell had said to Lambert in 1650, 'These very persons would
shout as much if you and I were going to be hanged.' Those who were
not pleased with the Restoration, Sir John Reresby shrewdly observed,
'durst not oppose the current by seeming otherwise' . . . .

By the Compromise of 1660 the idealists on both sides were sacrified.
Vane and Harrison were publicly disembowelled, Quakers and other
sectaries were driven into a harried underground existence: while on the
other hand many of the smaller Cavaliers got no compensation for their
losses and sufferings. Those who inherited the earth were hard-faced
businessmen like George Downing, who betrayed his comrades to the
executioner's knife and got a baronetcy; stolid professionals like George
Monck who became Duke of Albemarle ('some men will betray three
kingdoms for filthy lucre's sake', a minister said to his face); ex-
Presbyterians like William Prynne, who said, 'If Charles Stuart is to come
in, it were better for those that waged war against his father that he should
come in by their votes'; ex-Royalist ex-Cromwellians like Sir Anthony
Ashley-Cooper, an affluent member of Committees for Plantations
before and after 1660. 'The corrupt interests of the lawyers and clergy'
proved too strong for the radicals, and the ultimate victors in 1660 were
those conservatives who had been united against Laud and Strafford in
1640–1 and who came together again in face of a new threat to liberty
and property, this time from the many-headed monster and the Army of
the sectaries. The gentry were able to re-unite in 1660 because the lines of
civil war division were drawn within a class which had cultural ties and
social prejudices in common despite political, religious, and economic
aspirations. When in January 1660 the diarist John Evelyn tried to
persuade the Parliamentarian Governor of the Tower of London to
declare for the King, he noted that his negotiation was 'to the great hazard
of my life; but the Colonel had been my schoolfellow and I knew would
not betray me.' This early appearance of 'the old school tie' was symbolic.

Christopher Hill, *The Century of Revolution 1603–1714*, 1969,
pp 129–30, 166–7

Questions

a Why did Presbyterians, men of property and gentry unite in 1660 to invite back Charles II?

b In what ways does Hill imply a lack of sincerity amongst various groups and individuals who supported the Restoration?

* c Explain the historical significance of (i) 'They brought rumps for the populace to roast' (line 29) (ii) 'in 1623 they had paid for rejoicings at the return of Prince Charles from Spain' (lines 29 and 30) (iii) 'law reform, stable copyholds and other Leveller objectives' (line 5).

* d Why were Vane and Harrison 'publicly disembowelled' (line 36)? What was their historical importance?

* e Explain why the Presbyterians after the Restoration found themselves 'the despised and cheated party' (lines 9 and 10). (See also documents 5 and 6.)

3 Declaration of Breda 1660

Charles, by the grace of God, King of England, Scotland, France and Ireland, Defender of the Faith, etc. To all our loving subjects, of what degree or quality soever, greeting.

If the general distraction and confusion which is spread over the whole
5 Kingdom doth not awaken all men to a desire and longing that those wounds which have so many years together been kept bleeding, may be bound up, all we can say will be to no purpose; however, after this long silence, we have thought it our duty to declare how much we desire to contribute thereunto; . . . And to the end that the fear of punishment
10 may not engage any, conscious to themselves of what is past, to a perseverance in guilt for the future, by opposing the quiet and happiness of their country, in the restoration of King, Peers and people to their just, ancient and fundamental rights, we do, by these presents, declare, that we do grant a free and general pardon, which we are ready, upon demand, to
15 pass under our Great Seal of England, to all our subjects, of what degree or quality soever, who, within forty days after the publishing hereof, shall lay hold upon this our grace and favour, and shall, by any public act, declare their doing so, and that they return to the loyalty and obedience of good subjects; excepting only such persons as shall hereafter be excepted
20 by Parliament, those only to be excepted . . . we desiring and ordaining that henceforth all notes of discord, separation and difference of parties be utterly abolished among all our subjects, whom we invite and conjure to a perfect union among themselves, under our protection, for the re-settlement of our just rights and theirs in a free Parliament, by which,
25 upon the word of a King, we will be advised.

And because the passion and uncharitableness of the times have produced several opinions in religion, by which men are engaged in parties and animosities against each other (which, when they shall hereafter unite

in a freedom of conversation, will be composed or better understood), we
30 do declare a liberty to tender consciences, and that no man shall be
disquieted or called in question for difference of opinion in matter of
religion, which do not disturb the peace of the Kingdom; and that we
shall be ready to consent to such an Act of Parliament, as, upon mature
deliberation, shall be offered to us, for the full granting that indulgence.
35   And because in the continued distractions of so many years, and so
many and great revolutions, many grants and purchases of estates have
been made to and by many officers, soldiers and others, who are now
possessed of the same, and who may be liable to actions at law upon
several titles, we are likewise willing that all such differences, and all
40 things relating to such grants, sales and purchases, shall be determined in
Parliament, which can best provide for the satisfaction of all men who are
concerned . . . .
   Given under our Sign Manual and Privy Signet, at our Court at Breda
this 4/14 day of April, 1660, in the twelfth year of our reign.
   Declaration of Breda 1660

Questions

a   What, according to the king, was his *overall* purpose in this
    declaration?
b   What particular promises did the king make to his subjects concern-
    ing their three most worrying problems in facing a Restoration?
* c How far did he keep those promises during his reign?
d   What did he imply about the position of parliament and his
    relationship to it?

4   Republican Disapproval

The new King being suddenly expected, great numbers of those who had
been officers in the Cavalier army, or were otherwise zealous for him,
procured horses and cloths, for the most part upon credit, and formed
themselves into troops under the Lord Litchfield, Lord Cleveland, and
5 that apostate Brown the wood-monger, in order to attend him at his
reception. And news being brought that he was put out to sea, Monk,
accompanied with a guard of horse, marched to Dover, and received him
at his landing: the King embraced him, kissed him, and called him father;
and it might be truly said, that in some respects they were very nearly
10 allied. At Canterbury the King presented him with the George and
Garter; the first was put on by the Duke of York, the other by the Duke of
Gloucester. And because it was suspected that the army which fought
against him, might still retain some of their former inclinations: it was
resolved that the King, with his brothers, shall lodge at the house of
15 Colonel Gibbons, one of their officers, at Rochester. Many Knights were
made in this journey, and bonfires were to be seen in great numbers on the

road; the inconstant multitude in some places burning the badges of their own freedom, the arms of the Commonwealth. Monk's army was drawn up on Blackheath and by the best judges was thought to deserve the fool's
20 coat rather than the souldier's casaque.

The Lord Mayor, Sheriffs and Aldermen of the City, treated their King with a collation under a tent, placed in St. George's Fields; and five or six hundred citizens cloathed in coats of black velvet, and (not improperly) wearing chains about their necks, by an order of the
25 Common Council, attended on the triumph of that day; with much more empty pageantry which I purposely omit: but I must not pass over the folly and insolence manifested at that time by those who had been so often defeated in the field, and had contributed nothing either of bravery or policy to this change, in ordering the souldiery to ride with swords drawn
30 through the city of London to White Hall, the Duke of York and Monk leading the way; and intimating (as was supposed) a resolution to maintain that by force which had been obtained by fraud.

The Lords, with those who sate in the House of Commons, received the King at Whitehall after this tedious cavalcade, where the Speakers of
35 both Houses loaded him with complements; and took the best care they could to make him believe himself to be the best, greatest and bravest prince in the whole world . . . .

The dissolution and drunkenness of that night was so great and scandalous, in a nation which had not been acquainted with such
40 disorders for so many years past, that the King, who still stood in need of the Presbyterian party which had betray'd all into his hands, for their satisfaction, caused a proclamation to be publish'd, forbidding the drinking of healths. But resolving, for his own part, to be obliged to no rule of any kind, he publickly violated his own order in a few days, at a
45 debauch in the Mulberry Garden; and more privately at another meeting in the City, where he drank healths to the utmost excess till two in the morning.

C. H. Firth (ed.), *The Memoirs of Edmund Ludlow*, 1894, Vol II, pp 273—5

Questions

a   What opinion does Ludlow (a republican soldier and politician) hold of (i) ex-officers of the royalist army (ii) the new king (iii) the celebrations?

*   b   Explain how lines 17 and 18 lend support to an argument expressed by Hill in document 2.

*   c   In what way had the presbyterian party 'betray'd all into his hands' (line 41)?

d   How does Ludlow express his belief that the English people were surrendering their freedom for oppression?

5   Corporation Act 1661

. . . And be it further enacted . . . That all persons who upon the four
and twentieth day of December, one thousand six hundred and sixty and
one, shall be mayors, aldermen, recorders, bailiffs, town clerks, common
council-men, and other persons then bearing any office or offices of
5   magistracy, or places, or trusts, or other employment relating to or
concerning the government of the said respective cities, corporations, and
boroughs, and cinque ports, and their members, and other port towns,
shall at any time before the five and twentieth day of March, one
thousand six hundred sixty and three, when they shall be thereunto
10 required by the said respective commissioners or any three of them, take
the Oaths of Allegiance and Supremacy, and this oath following:

> I, A.B., do declare and believe, That it is not lawful, upon any pretence
> whatsoever, to take arms against the King; and that I do abhor that traitorous
> position of taking arms by his authority against his person, or against those that
15 are commissioned by him: So help me God.

And also at the same time shall publicly subscribe before the said
commissioners or any three of them the following declaration:

> I, A.B., do declare that I hold that there lies no obligation upon me or any other
> person from the oath commonly called the Solemn League and Covenant, and
20 that the same was in itself an unlawful oath and imposed upon the subjects of
> this realm against the known laws and liberties of the Kingdom.

And that all such of the said mayors and other the persons
aforesaid . . . Who shall refuse to take and subscribe the same within the
time and in manner aforesaid shall from and immediately after such
25 refusal be by authority of this Act (*ipso facto*) removed and displaced of
and from the said offices and places respectively . . . .
   Provided also . . . That from and after the expiration of the said
commissions, no person or persons shall for ever hereafter be placed,
elected or chosen, in or to any the offices or places aforesaid, that shall not
30 have, within one year next before such election or choice, taken the
sacrament of the Lord's Supper, according to the rites of the Church of
England . . . .
   Corporation Act 1661

Questions

*   *a*   Explain the historical background which caused parliament to include
    the non-resistance oath (lines 12−15) in this Act.
*   *b*   Explain the historical background to 'the oath commonly called the
    Solemn League and Covenant' (line 19).
  c   Why would Presbyterians find it difficult to meet the requirements of
    the Corporation Act?
  d   Do the Act of Uniformity (see document 6) and the Corporation Act

in any way break or maintain the promises made in the Declaration of Breda (document 3)?

6 Act of Uniformity 1662

... Some few alterations were made in the liturgy by the Bishops themselves: a few new collects were made, as the prayer for all conditions of men, and the general thanksgiving. A collect was also drawn for the Parliament, in which a new epithet was added to the King's title, that
5 gave great offence, and occasioned much indecent raillery: he was stiled our most religious King. It was not easy to give a proper sense to this, and to make it go well down; since whatever signification of religion might be in the *Latin* word, as importing the sacredness of the King's person, yet, in the *English* language, it bore a signification that was in no way
10 applicable to the King. And those who took great liberties with him, have often asked him, what must all his people think, when they heard him prayed for as their most religious King? Some other lesser additions were made. But care was taken, that nothing should be altered, so as it had been moved by the Presbyterians, for it was resolved to gratify them in
15 nothing . . . .

The act passed by no great majority: and by it all who did not conform to the liturgy by the twenty fourth of August, St. *Bartholomew's* day, in the year 1662, were deprived of all ecclesiastical benefices, without leaving any discretional power with the King in the execution of it, and
20 without making provision for the maintenance of those who should be so deprived: a severity neither practised by Queen Elizabeth in the enacting her liturgy, nor by Cromwell in ejecting the Royalists, in both which, a fifth part of the benefice was reserved for their subsistence! St. Bartholomew's day was pitched on, that, if they were then deprived, they
25 should lose the profits of the whole year, since the tithes are commonly due at Michaelmas. The Presbyterians remembered what a St. Bartholomew's had been held at Paris ninety years before, which was the day of that massacre, and did not stick to compare the one to the other. The book of Common Prayer with the new corrections, was that to
30 which they were to subscribe . . . But the Presbyterians were now in great difficulties. They had many meetings, and much disputing about conformity. Reynolds accepted the bishopric of Norwich. But Calamy and Baxter refused the sees of Litchfield and Hereford. And about two thousand of them fell under the parliamentary deprivation, as they gave
35 out. The numbers have been much controverted.

Bishop Burnet, *History of His Own Time*, 1753, Vol I, pp 266–9

Questions

a Why did the new prayer for parliament (lines 3 and 4) cause so much comment? (See also document 3 and section IX).

b What was the main point in the Act of Uniformity? Why was 24 August chosen as the deadline date?

* *c* Explain the historical significance of (i) 'nor by Cromwell in ejecting the Royalists' (line 22) (ii) what a St. Bartholomew's had been held at Paris ninety years before' (lines 26 and 27).

* *d* What were the consequences of the Act?

IX Charles II and the Historians

Introduction

Interpretations of the reign of Charles II and the personality of the king himself have varied considerably since the seventeenth century. How far should we believe the evidence of some of his contemporaries who knew him well – men like the earl of Clarendon, Bishop Burnet and Samuel Pepys? By them he is portrayed as a lazy, pleasure-seeking cynic, who neglected public business at considerable cost to the nation. How creditable, on the other hand, is the Whig interpretation of this period, advocated in the nineteenth century first by Lord Macaulay and later by George Trevelyan? This put forward the theory of a plot, cunningly devised by Charles, to establish a new Stuart despotism based on the catholic religion and backed by French arms. If we reject this view, how can we explain the Secret Treaty of Dover (1670) in which Charles promised to declare his own conversion to Catholicism? How much personal responsibility should be attached to the king for setting Louis XIV and France on the road to conquest and glory? Finally, how convincing are modern re-appraisals which have taken into account recent research based on administrative records? These are a few of the issues raised in this section. The extracts chosen perhaps illustrate most vividly that it is extremely difficult for any historian, whenever born, to escape from his own personal prejudices and those of the age in which he lives. They illustrate, too, the problems of perspective encountered by contemporary historians (like Burnet), as well as the risks of 'wisdom through hindsight' by those who write later (like Trevelyan).

Further Reading

Maurice Ashley, *Charles II* (Praeger, New York, 1971)
Arthur Bryant, *King Charles II* (Longman, 1955 ed.)
K. H. D. Haley, *Charles II* (Historical Association Pamphlet, 1966)
C. H. Hartmann, *The King My Brother* (Heinemann, 1954)
G. M. Trevelyan, *England Under the Stuarts* (Methuen, 1904).

1 A Bishop's View

The King was then thirty years of age, and, as might have been supposed,
past the levities of youth, and the extravagance of pleasure. He had a very
good understanding. He knew well the state of affairs both at home and
abroad. He had a softness of temper that charmed all who came near him,
5   till they found how little they could depend on good looks, kind words,
and fair promises; in which he was liberal to excess, because he intended
nothing by them, but to get rid of importunities, and to silence all further
pressing upon him. He seemed to have no sense of religion: both at
prayers and sacrament, he, as it were, took care to satisfy people, that he
10 was in no sort concerned in that about which he was employed. So that he
was very far from being an hypocrite, unless his assisting at those
performances, was a sort of hypocrisy (as no doubt it was): but he was sure
not to increase that by any the least appearance of religion. He said once to
myself, that he was no Atheist, but he could not think God would make a
15 man miserable only for taking a little pleasure out of the way. He
disguised his Popery to the last. But when he talked freely, he could not
help letting himself out against the liberty that, under the reformation, all
men took of inquiring into matters of religion: for, from their inquiring
into matters of religion they carried the humour farther to inquire into
20 matters of state. He said often, he thought government was a much safer
and easier thing where the authority was believed infallible, and the faith
and submission of the people was implicit: about which I had once much
discourse with him. He had much compass of knowledge tho' he was
never capable of much application or study. He understood the
25 mechanicks and physick, and was a good chymist, and much set on
several preparations of mercury, chiefly the fixing it. He understood
navigation well: but, above all, he knew the architecture of ships so
perfectly, that, in that respect, he was exact rather more than became a
prince. He was an everlasting talker . . . . He thought that nobody did
30 serve him out of love: and so he was quits with all the world, and loved
others as little as he thought they loved him. He hated business, and could
not be easily brought to mind any: but, when it was necessary, and he was
set to it, he would stay as long as his ministers had work for him. The ruin
of his reign, and of all his affairs, was occasioned chiefly by his delivering
35 himself up at his first coming over to a mad range of pleasure. One of the
race of the Villars . . . who was advanced to be Duchess of Cleveland,
was his first and longest mistress, by whom he had five children. She was
a woman of great beauty, but most enormously vicious and
ravenous . . . . His passion for her, and her strange behaviour towards
40 him, did so disorder him, that often he was not master of himself, nor
capable of minding business, which in so critical a time required great
application . . . .

Bishop Burnet, *History of His Own Time*, 1753, Vol 1, pp 130–2

Questions

a What good qualities does Burnet see in Charles II?

b Why had the king been critical of the religious freedom which had been produced by the Reformation?

c Which particular aspect of the king's character does Burnet blame for the misfortunes of the reign? (Compare this with Hume's opinion in document 2).

d In what ways does Burnet's own personal prejudice against the king show itself in this extract and colour his judgement?

2 A Tory View

If we survey the character of Charles the Second in the different lights, which it will admit of, it will appear very various, and give rise to different and even opposite sentiments. When considered as a companion, he appears the most amiable and engaging of men; and indeed, in this
5   view, his deportment must be allowed altogether unexceptionable. His love of raillery was so tempered with good breeding, that it was never offensive . . . . This indeed is the most shining part of the King's character; and he seems to have been sensible of it: For he was fond of dropping the formality of state, and of relapsing every moment into the
10 companion.

    In the duties of private life, his conduct, tho' not free from exception, was, in the main, laudable. He was an easy generous lover, a civil obliging husband, a friendly brother, an indulgent father, and a good natured master . . . .
15   With a detail of his private character we must set bounds to our panegyric on Charles. The other parts of his conduct may admit of some apology, but can deserve small applause . . . . When we consider him as a Sovereign, his character, tho' not altogether void of virtues, was in the main dangerous to his people, and dishonourable to himself. Negligent of
20 the interests of the nation, careless of its glory, averse to its religion, jealous of its liberty, lavish of its treasure, sparing only of its blood; he exposed it by his measures, tho' he appeared ever but in sport, to the danger of a furious civil war, and even to the ruin and ignominy of a foreign conquest. Yet may all these enormities, if fairly and candidly
25 examined, be imputed, in a great measure, to the indolence of his temper; a fault, which, however unfortunate in a Monarch, it is impossible for us to regard with great severity. It has been remarked of this King, that he never said a foolish thing, nor even did a wise one . . . .

    But his attachment to France, after all the pains, which we have taken,
30 by enquiry and conjecture, to fathom it, contains still something, it must be confessed, mysterious and inexplicable. The hopes of rendering himself absolute by Lewis's assistance seem so chimerical, that they could scarce be retained with such obstinacy by a Prince of Charles's

penetration: And as to pecuniary subsidies, he surely spent much greater
sums in one season, during the second Dutch war, then were remitted
from France during the course of his whole reign. I am apt therefore to
imagine, that Charles was in this particular guided chiefly by inclination,
and by a prepossession in favour of the French nation. He considered that
people as gay, sprightly, polite, elegant, courteous, devoted to their
Prince, and attached to the catholic faith; and for these reasons he
cordially loved them.

David Hume, *The History of England*, 1767, Vol VIII, pp 204–7

Questions

a Why is Hume not surprised that people have formed very differing
views of Charles II?

b Which particular aspect of the king's character does Hume blame for
the misfortunes of the reign?

* c From your knowledge of the period explain how Charles II exposed
the country 'to the danger of a furious civil war' (line 23).

* d How does Hume's explanation of the motives behind the French
alliance differ from that given by Trevelyan (see document 3)?

* e Would you say that Hume offers here a typical Tory view of the king?

3 A Whig View

. . . Ever since 1662, his intrigue for the temporary Toleration of Dissent
had been the by-play of his plot for the permanent restoration of
Catholicism. The secret motive of Charles's actions, unknown to the
knavish ministers who thought that because he was their boon companion he was also their fool, unknown in after years to generations of
Englishmen who laughed over and loved the memory of their merry
monarch, was his design to erect a Second Stuart Despotism, far more
terrible in its nature than the First Despotism which his grandfather had
inherited and his father lost. The hero of the tennis-court and the
ballroom, whom no one in Whitehall respected and no one but his Queen
feared; the King of idleness who set on his Councillors to mimic their
rivals like schoolboys; the humorist whose thick licentious lips were a
fountain of wit, seemingly his only defence against servants who robbed
and statesmen who opposed him; the hunter of moths, the friend of little
dogs, was plotting an overthrow of our religion, our liberties and even
our racial independence, far more revolutionary than the papal vassalage
into which old barbarous England had once been sold by its grim King
John. Charles II was negotiating treaties with Louis XIV to subvert
Protestantism and to establish personal government in Britain by the help
of French arms.

The plan of the Second or Catholic Stuart Despotism was long thought
to have been due to the personal insanity of James II for he alone put it

in force; but Charles originated the idea, and though he afterwards abandoned it, he handed it on to his less able brother. It was based on
25 Catholicism, Toleration, a standing army and the French alliance. Herein it differed from the First Despotism of Laud's and Strafford's master, who had been hostile both to Popery and Toleration, and undecided in his attempts to possess a regular army or to obtain help from France. Charles I took his stand on custom, and therefore relied on prestige; Charles II
30 attempted revolution, and therefore relied on force . . . .

It remained to be seen what the Tories and the Monarchy would make of England. Their first step was to destroy local self-government. The charters of many of the principal cities were challenged and declared forfeit on frivolous grounds by Chief Justice Jeffreys; while numbers of
35 other towns, great and small, hastened to prevent the confiscation by the voluntary surrender of their privileges. The King restored the charters in new forms, which put the municipalities into the hands of his own nominees. No such thing had ever happened before in England . . . . It was no part even of Strafford's policy of 'thorough', that the power of the
40 sovereign should be extended to municipal affairs, or to the nomination of members of Parliament . . . .

The second Stuart despotism had come into being. It was based, as Charles had designed in 1670, on a standing army and on the financial help of France. Yet he had realised only half the ideas of the Dover Treaty.
45 For the supreme power which he enjoyed was connected, not with Roman Catholicism and the purchase of Nonconformist support, but with Anglicanism and ferocious persecution of Dissent. The King had bought the Tories at a price. If Charles's successor would continue to pay that price, to extirpate the Nonconformists and depress the Catholics, the
50 despotism wielded in the interest of the squires might be confirmed by time and become the established constitution of the realm. But if an attempt were made to convert it into a Catholic despotism, there would be hope for England yet.

G. M. Trevelyan, *England under the Stuarts*, 1904, pp 365–6, 424–5

Questions

a Explain, in full, what Trevelyan means by the 'Second Stuart Despotism' (line 7).

* b From your knowledge of the period, what do you understand by 'the First Despotism which his grandfather had inherited and his father lost' (lines 8 and 9)?

* c In what sense had Charles II 'realised only half the ideas of the Dover Treaty' (line 44)?

* d In what way does Trevelyan differ from Bryant (see document 4) in his interpretation of the surrender of borough charters (lines 31–41)?

e How does Trevelyan reveal in this extract his own political prejudice against Charles II?

4 A Twentieth-Century View

Three years had now elapsed since England had seen a Parliament, and some of those about the King – notably Halifax and Ormonde – urged that he should rely on the change in public opinion to honour the old Triennial Act and call one. But York was bitterly opposed, and Charles himself felt little enthusiasm for reassembling that house of talkers, from which he and his father had suffered so much. He was at peace at last and his people united, trade was flourishing, he was beginning to make both ends meet: why should he venture on seas that had proved so often dangerous for the sake of a dubious and theoretic good? So long as Louis paid his modest subsidy, he could manage without calling on his people for new taxes – they were the richer so and he the more at ease . . . .

To his people, the last years of Charles's reign brought a wonderful prosperity. While Europe was plunged in war, they remained at peace, both with themselves and their neighbours. 'Then', recalled Lord Ailesbury, writing in a more costly age, 'we had no generals to march themselves at the head of superfluous armies, nor had we one penny raised on land tax.' Yet the very force and treasure which England poured out so lavishly in the wars of Marlborough, she drew from these quiet years when King Charles was leading her through green pastures. Everywhere men were laying up for themselves and their children treasure for the future . . . . In a quarter of a century, Evelyn's £250, invested in the stock of the East India Company, had multiplied itself threefold. Pennsylvania, whither Charles had dispatched the Quaker Penn in 1682, the Carolinas, New York and the shores of the Hudson; treaties with the Turks and the Moors to make Englishmen free of the Mediterranean; trading settlements at Bombay and Fort William, and dusky ambassadors bringing gifts from the great Mogul; companies to trade with Africa, Guinea and the coasts of Barbary; expeditions to find a new road to the golden East through the Arctic ice or discover the wonders of the South Seas: all these were milestones in England's commercial and imperial expansion, and all, in their greater or lesser degree, bore the impress of a Prince, who once told his sister: 'The thing which is nearest the heart of this nation is trade and all that belongs to it' . . . .

In all this, Charles helped to create a newer and richer England and instil into the minds of his subjects a love of a more spacious and pleasant mode of life than they had known before. The very luxury of his Court had served to bring this about . . . . The glories of Windsor and Greenwich, the new faubourg of St. James, and the London which arose from the ashes of the fire, posterity owes primarily to him. Everywhere his subjects followed his example, building those commodious and classical houses which in the next age were to give a park and palace to every village in England, encompassing gardens with walls to catch the sunlight, making fountains and parterres and grottoes, and planting walks of ash and sycamore . . . .

Charles was now master of as great a power as any King of England

had wielded — the sweeter that it was founded, with little help of arms or money, on his people's love . . . . In the last passionate revival of loyalty to the ancient throne, it seemed as though English political liberty, fought for so long and fiercely, was to be thrown aside as a thing of no worth
50 beside the greater blessing of a King at one with his people. When Jeffreys took the Northern Assize that summer, charter after charter was laid at his feet, to be altered or amended as his master chose. To immortalise the King's glory, the London merchants set up his statute in their Exchange, sculptured by Grinling Gibbons and arrayed in the habit of a Roman
55 Caesar.

Never had the English people known such a King: the frailties of his life were now coloured by the kindly hand of time, the political bitterness of a few years back forgotten, his enemies discredited or in hiding. There was nothing remote or inaccessible about this British Titus — receiving
60 ambassadors amid the unchecked throng of his subjects, feeding his ducks while all the world watched, pulling off his hat to the meanest as he took his walk in the park or galleries . . . . Yet, though he had words at will and knew the art of pleasing, so well that he would send away a petitioner enchanted by the mere charm of his reception, he could, when he chose,
65 by a mere change of countenance, put on a terrible majesty . . . .

Arthur Bryant, *King Charles II*, 1931, pp 344–7, 349–50

Questions

a What particular benefits, according to Bryant, did Charles II bring to the English people in the last years of his reign?

* b Explain what you understand by 'the old Triennial Act' (lines 3 and 4). What reasons are advanced here for the king's refusal to honour it and for the people's apparent willingness to throw aside their 'political liberty' (line 48)?

* c Who were the 'enemies discredited or in hiding' (line 58)?

d How does Bryant excuse the extravagance of Charles's court?

* e Compare Bryant's style of writing history with that of Trevelyan (see document 3).

5 Views Reconciled

The conclusions of historians change over the years, not only as a result of the discovery of new evidence, but as a result of the changing times in which historians themselves live and work. We have become familiar with the notion that each generation of historians may have its own
5 questions to ask, its own standards and conscious or unconscious preconceptions by which to judge. The historical reputation of Charles II is a fascinating example of this. Broadly speaking, opinions about him may be divided into two sharply contrasting groups . . . .

The two pictures furnish as great a contract as could be imagined. In its

10 most extreme form, the traditional view represents Charles as a cynical, disillusioned rake, coming back from exile in 1660 resolved to enjoy himself and, in the words of that most famous of all historical cliches, 'never to go on his travels again'. Having no ideals himself, he set a notoriously bad example in a particularly dissipated Court in the pursuit
15 of personal pleasures; his immorality and extravagance continued against a background of imprisoned Puritan preachers and unpaid starving seamen thronging the London streets in the second Dutch War. His laziness and inattentiveness to public affairs were illustrated from the pages of Clarendon or from Pepÿs's pictures of 'the silliness of the King,
20 playing with his dog all the while, and not minding the business' in Council or (though this story is not first hand) having supper with Lady Castlemaine and hunting a moth round the room while the Dutch fleet sailed up the River Medway. He was accused of calling Parliament as little as he could, ignoring its advice and bribing its members. He
25 accepted French money in secret to pursue a highly dishonourable foreign policy in support of Louis XIV; and the Secret Treat of Dover of 1670 included promises of French assistance in men and money for schemes to promote royal absolutism and Roman Catholicism in England. Sometimes, it may be added, condemnations of the Treaty of
30 Dover were not altogether consistent with the accompanying charges of laziness and cynicism.

In this view of Charles's character the most that he could be credited with was a genuine love of the sea and an interest in the fortunes of the English navy, together with a certain low cunning which in the end
35 allowed him to get the better of the Whigs and to end his reign in full authority over a loyal and subservient people. But, this apart, the fortunes of England under this self-indulgent ruler were at a low ebb: Britannia on the coins had the features of one of the ladies at Court, Frances Stuart, while the Medway episode represented the greatest naval disgrace in
40 British history. Louis XIV was allowed to pursue his way unchallenged on the Continent, while at home there was chronic maladministration, embezzlement, friction and disharmony between the King and the elected representatives of his people.

The rival view of 'Good King Charles's golden days' challenged this
45 picture in several ways. Firstly, new facts came to light, expecially the discovery by Dr. W. A. Shaw that Charles's financial position would have been impossible quite apart from his own personal extravagance or his lavish grants to his mistresses. The House of Commons failed to provide sufficient money for the government's genuine needs . . . . The
50 financial stituation was made even worse by the depression caused by war and the natural disasters of the Plague and Fire of London, and Dr. Shaw's conclusion was that it would have been hopeless even with the best possible management of the resources available. It could be argued that it was the chronic shortage of money which was basically responsible for
55 the great disasters of the reign, such as those of the Second Dutch War. Dr. Shaw went further, and contended that it was the niggardliness of the

House of Commons, and its failure to answer the King's legitimate demands, that drove Charles to negotiate for subsidies from Louis XIV and
thus came to dominate his foreign policy. All this may be taken as an
60 illustration of the way in which the increased study of official records,
made possible by easier access to state archives, had led generally to a
greater sense of the difficulties and the responsibilities of government.
Whereas at one time opposition criticisms (and particularly those
recorded by memoir-writers) were accepted at their face value, it had
65 become possible to detect in them much ignorance, irresponsibility,
prejudice, and sometimes interested motives . . . .

Another change of attitude also influenced the view which was taken
by Charles. The mood of disillusionment with great political and
religious issues, and the mood of moral self-indulgence which were so
70 prevalent in the 1660s fitted in well enough with the post-war 1918
period. Charles's lack of idealism, his mistresses and fourteen officially
recognized illegitimate children no longer excited the same disap-
probation. Like Pepys he was now regarded with some affection as an
amusing old rascal, very 'human' in his failings, and it was even possible
75 for Sir Arthur Bryant to argue that anyway Charles's 'affectionate
generosity to his bastard sons . . . was no more costly to the country
than the normal brood of younger princes denied them by a childless
queen'. This is not an argument which one would have expected to find
used by a Victorian historian . . . . At a time when the long national
80 enmity between England and France had been replaced by the *entente
cordiale* of the twentieth century, the idea was also put forward, notably
by Mr. C. H. Hartmann, that the French alliance of 1670 was not really as
disastrous as older historians had made out, but was a master-stroke of
diplomacy against England's commercial and naval rivals, the Dutch,
85 who, it was alleged, were the real national enemy in 1670. On these
grounds the Secret Treaty of Dover, ignominious failure though it was,
was described as a 'brilliant foreign policy'; and Charles was portrayed as
a great King, who, far from tamely submitting to be Louis XIV's
pensioner, by sheer diplomatic skill managed to make use of Louis XIV for
90 English interests . . . .

Perhaps the safest conclusion might be that although the graver charges
of the Whig historians against him were exaggerated, he cannot
convincingly be built up into anything like a great monarch.

K. H. D. Haley, 'Charles II, in *The Stuarts*, 1973, pp 134−8, 153

Questions

a   Why do the views of historians change over the years? (See also
section IV). Can historical truth ever be attained?

b   Which of the previous extracts have portrayed Chales II as (i) cynical
(line 10) (ii) inattentive to public affairs (line 18) (iii) full of
low cunning (line 34) (iv) given over to personal pleasures (line 15)?

c   Why did it become possible for later historians in the twentieth century to take a more tolerant view of Charles II's (i) treaty with France (ii) immorality?

* *d* Explain what you understand by (i) 'the pages of Clarendon' (line 19) (ii) 'the Medway episode' (line 39).

X The Glorious Revolution 1688

Introduction

In 1685 James II had inherited a parliament which was noticeably Tory, a church which preached the duty of non-resistance and a people who clearly wished to be loyal. Within three years, all this had been squandered. Parliament, alienated by the menacing army on Hounslow Heath under newly-appointed catholic officers, petitioned against it — and was promptly dismissed. The church, alienated by the appointment of Catholics to his office and by the Declaration of Indulgence (1687), petitioned against the policy — and seven bishops were promptly imprisoned. The people, fearful that the birth of a son to James (1688) would mean the establishment of a permanent catholic despotism, invited across William of Orange as defender of their rights. The Revolution had commenced.

Important questions, however, need to be raised. Did James have the legal right to pass the Declaration of Indulgence? What were his real motives in the weeks prior to his flight? Did he seriously plan to plunge the country into anarchy? Was he, by this time, largely insane or merely frightened out of his wits? Why did the Whigs and Tories suddenly sink their differences? What part did William play in securing the throne for himself? Historians have disagreed in answering these questions, as the following extracts will show.

Gilbert Burnet, the author of the second extract, had aroused the enmity of James by his sermons against popery and his friendship with Lord Willian Russell. Wisely choosing to go abroad on the accession of James in 1685, he joined the court of William and Mary in Holland. There he became a close friend of the future king, advising him on his policy towards the invitation and accompanying him on his expedition to England. He was rewarded by being appointed bishop of Salisbury.

Further Reading

Stephen B. Baxter, *William III* (Long.nan, 1966)
Jock Haswell, *James II, Soldier and Sailor* (St Martin's, New York, 1972).
G. J. Renier, *William of Orange* (Nelson 1932)
G. M. Trevelyan, *The English Revolution, 166–1689* (Butterworth, 1938)
F. C. Turner, *James II* (Eyre and Spottiswoode, 1948)

1   The Flight of James II

Why did James II leave his Kingdom on December 22nd, 1688, having already failed in an earlier attempt? Was there a positive plan; or was it merely the ultimate folly of a madman who hoped to throw England into anarchy? Originally put forward by Maculay and older historians, this theory has been accepted by more recent authorities, led by Trevelyan and Feiling. Christopher Hill's neo-Whig interpretation of the flight is that it was simply an 'appeal to anarchy'. Or was it, after all, pure cowardice on the part of a frustrated and demented man? Although David Ogg regards the whole inquiry as probably futile, he asserts that James was unable to formulate any clear plan and thus ran away. None of these explanations is entirely satisfactory; all tend to suggest the wrong motives or no motive at all. If there be an answer, the clue lies not so much in the mere failure of his policies – which, even to James, must have been patent before the shattering acquittal of the Seven Bishops (June 30th, 1688) – as in his inability to reconcile the consequences of such failure with his ossified political beliefs . . . . James II had failed before the Revolution began. Yet he remained King – *de jure, de facto*; and to one indoctrinated with theories of Divine Right, nothing but death could alter that. It was his awareness of this apparently unassailable position that caused him to commit the tactical error of flight.

The weeks preceding the landing of William on November 5th were full or rumour and action. Finally convinced that the Dutch naval preparations were a prelude to invasion, James appeared shaken and irritable. His nerve held, however, and he displayed his usual hostility to those courtiers who tried to prove him wrong . . . . The landing at Brixham was unopposed . . . . James was forced to counter; after some indecision, he had prepared for defence and was in camp at Salisbury, where a debilitating nose-bleed was the least of his troubles. Morale was low; and on November 23rd, John Churchill, who owed everything to James, deserted to William. Two days later, when James was on his way back to London, Sarah Churchill was ushering Princess Anne to Bishop Compton's residence en route for the North.

At this point, when the Revolution begins to impinge upon a mind perhaps already unbalanced, it is convenient to consider the first charge of cowardice against James. Instead of retiring, he could have remained at Salisbury or advanced to give battle to William in the west . . . . From what we know of his earlier years, James did not lack courage. In exile he had trained and fought under Turenne, who held a very high opinion of him as man and soldier. Later, on several occasions when his duties as Lord High Admiral took him on board ship, James showed abilities far superior to those of any other Stuart. Indeed, he was the hero of the Second Dutch War, and was voted £120,000 by Parliament 'in token of the great sense they had of his conduct and bravery'. On May 6th, 1642, when the *Gloucester* was wrecked on its voyage to Scotland, it was not his cowardice that James's critics noted, but his callous concern for the safety of his own popish entourage and his dog rather than for the survival of the crew. And within nine days of that disaster James was at sea again. The reason why he did not stand his ground at Salisbury, or later, was not cowardice but a sudden and stunning discovery that he could no longer command the loyalty of the troops whom he had once drilled to perfection on Hounslow Heath. When he eventually decided to escape, the King mentioned this disaffection and the obsolescence of his army; his mind had been made up when Feversham and the others 'had told me that it was no ways advisable to venture myself at their head' . . . .

Meanwhile, James had received early warning of William's terms; and on the 11th he himself left London, only to be arrested at Faversham by a group of fishermen on the look-out for fugitive Catholics. Unrecognised, the 'hatchet-faced old Jesuit' was ill-treated and robbed, before being rescued and taken to an inn, where complaints at his lack of clean linen have been cited as evidence of his state of mind. But if James was mad, his madness was spasmodic; for to the end of his life he would enjoy long periods of relative sanity. When he was brought back to London on December 16th, he held a Privy Council as though flight had never even been contemplated. By December 14th William had reached Windsor; and, when he heard of the abortive flight, he did his best to ensure that James should not return to the capital . . . . On December 19th, James complied; he moved to Gravesend, where he stopped overnight before completing the journey to Sir Richard Head's house at Rochester. It was from here, during the early hours of the 23rd, that James made good his escape — he was in France in time for Christmas . . . .

It suited the Whig theory of total abdication to emphasize the absence of restraint on James and his freedom of choice during the final days; or, as Burnet put it: 'It was thought necessary to stick to the point of the King's deserting his people.' Fieling follows the line of many later historians when he asserts that James 'abandoned a people struggling to be loyal'. But there are several indications, noted by Macaulay and Trevelyan, that pressure may have been applied by William in an effort to scare James into flight . . . .

To prevent the summoning of a Parliament bent on diminishing his sovereignty, James threw the Great Seal into the Thames. It is this theatrical gesture, and his disbanding of the royal army without pay, that historians have presented as proof of James's anarchical motives ∵ . . . The removal of the Great Seal itself was probably more significant for James than for anyone else; certainly William was unconcerned. For the King the Seal was symbolic — an essential and integral part of traditional sovereignty, as was the Coronation Ring which he also removed. And by withdrawing not only these but also the person of the Monarch himself, he hoped to be able to prevent a radical change in government. He failed to understand that substitutes would do quite as well. His entire political philosophy was out of date, being established on fundamental principles of Divine Right inherited from James 1 and Charles 1, and nourished, during his earlier years, by the first

Earl of Clarendon's antique conception of a merely co-operative Parliament. It is characteristic of James's inability to learn from the past that Clarendon's fall, in large part due to Parliament's refusal to remain subservient, meant nothing to him . . . . To the day of his own death in 1701, James II remained true to the doctrines of Divine Right: the first article of the 'King's Advice' to his son, the Pretender, reads like a quotation from the works of James I: 'Kings are Accountable to none but to God alone for their Actions.' This is the simplest explanation of James's downfall. For too long he had been shielded from reality; and could never have admitted, even if he had understood, that Parliament was ultimately sovereign. It needed the Revolution and years of exile to show him that an absence *de jure* King was an embarrassment, but no obstacle, to a *de facto* ruler, enthroned by Parliamentary authority. Thus James II fled his realm, not for the purpose of producing anarchy, but because to his atrophied mind flight seemed the only means of stemming the flood of political action – or simply, of remaining King on his own uncompromising terms . . . . He hoped that from France he might negotiate from a position of strength, and never doubted that he would be allowed to return 'whensoever the Nation's Eyes shall be opened'. But, tactics aside, there appears to have been a more compelling reason for leaving England – he was convinced that his enemies really wished him dead . . . . It is difficult to understand why so few historians have been willing to see this human instinct in his parting words to Ailesbury: 'If I do not retire I shall certainly be sent to the Tower, and no King ever went out of that place but to his grave.'

A. A. Mitchell, *The Revolution of 1688 and the flight of James II* (in *History Today*, July 1965, pp 496, 499–504)

Questions

a   Explain, from the passage as a whole, why Mitchell feels that James committed 'the tactical error of flight' (line 20). What caused him to do so?

b   Why are (i) cowardice (ii) insanity rejected as factors in James's escape?

c   What main theory is normally advanced by Whig historians to explain James's motives in fleeing? What evidence do they use?

*   *d*   From your knowledge of his reign, is it true to say that James II was unable 'to learn from the past' (line 94)?

*   *e*   Compare his attitudes and policies with those of James I (see also section I).

2   The Motives of William of Orange

During all these debates, and the great heat with which they were managed, the Prince's own behaviour was very mysterious. He staid at

St. James's: he went little abroad: access to him was not very easy. He heard all that was said to him; but seldom made any answers. He did not affect to be affable or popular; nor would he take any pains to gain any one person over to his party. He said, he came over, being invited, to save the nation: he had now brought together a free and true representative of the Kingdom: he left it therefore to them to do what they thought best for the good of the Kingdom: and, when things were once settled, he should be well satisfied to go back to Holland again. Those who did not know him well, and who imagined that a crown had charms which human nature was not strong enough to resist, looked on all this as an affectation, and as a disguised threatning; which imported, that he would leave the nation to perish, unless this method of settling it was followed. After a reservedness that had continued to close for several weeks, that no body could certainly tell what he desired, he called for the Marquis of Halifax, and the Earls of Shrewsbury and Danby, and some others, to explain himself more distinctly to them.

He told them, he had been till then silent, because he would not say or do anything that might seem in any sort to take from any person the full freedom of deliberating and voting in matters of such importance: he was resolved neither to court nor to threaten anyone: and therefore he had declined to give out his own thoughts. Some were for putting the government in the hands of a Regent: he would say nothing against it, if it was thought the best mean for settling their affairs: only he thought it necessary to tell them, that he would not be the Regent: so, if they continued in that design, they must look out for some other person to be put in that post: he himself saw what the consequences of it were like to prove: so he would not accept of it. Others were for putting the Princess singly on the throne, and that he should reign by her courtesy: he said, no man could esteem a woman more than he did the Princess; but he was so made, that he could not think of holding any thing by apron-strings; nor could he think it reasonable to have any share in the government, unless it was put in his person, and that for term of life: if they did not think it fit to settle it otherwise, he would not oppose them in it: but he would go back to Holland, and meddle no more in their affairs. He assured them, that whatsoever others might think of a crown, it was no such thing in his eyes, but that he could live very well, and be well pleased without it. In the end he said, that he could not resolve to accept of a dignity, so as to hold it only on the life of another: yet he thought, that the issue of Princess Anne should be preferred in the succession, to any issue that he might have by any other wife than the Princess. All this he delivered to them, in so cold and unconcerned a manner, that those who judged of others by the dispositions that they felt in themselves, looked on it all as artifice and contrivance.

Bishop Burnet, *History of His Own Time*, 1753, Vol III, pp 297–8

Questions

a Why did some people look on William's attitude as 'a disguised threatning' (line 13)?

b How did William himself explain his prolonged silence?

* *c* Is there anything here to suggest that *Burnet* felt that William was completely sincere in what he said? Does your further reading suggest that William had other motives?

d What do we learn about William's character from this extract?

* *e* Explain fully the historical context of (i) 'Some were for putting the government in the hands of a Regent' (lines 23 and 24) (ii) 'Others were for putting the Princess singly on the throne' (lines 29 and 30) (iii) 'the issue of Princess Anne should be preferred in the succession' ' (lines 40 and 41).

3 The Bill of Rights 1689

. . . And whereas the said late King James II having abdicated the government, and the throne being thereby vacant, his Highness the Prince of Orange (whom it hath pleased Almighty God to make the glorious instrument of delivering this Kingdom from popery and
5 arbitrary power) did (by the advice of the Lords Spiritual and Temporal, and diverse principal persons of the Commons) cause letters to be written to the Lords Spiritual and Temporal, being Protestants, and other letters to the several counties, cities, universities, boroughs, and cinque ports, for the choosing of such persons as represent them, as were of right to be sent
10 to Parliament, to meet and sit at Westminster . . . And thereupon the said Lords Spiritual and Temporal, and Commons . . . do . . . declare:
1. That the pretended power of suspending laws, or the execution of laws, by regal authority, without consent of parliament, is illegal.
2. That the pretended power of dispensing with laws, or the execution of
15 laws by regal authority, as it hath been assumed and exercised of late, is illegal.
3. That the commission for erecting the late Court of Commissioners for Ecclesiastical causes, and all other commissions and courts of like nature, are illegal and pernicious.
20 4. That levying money for or to the use of the Crown, by pretence of prerogative, without grant of parliament, for longer time or in other manner than the same is or shall be granted, is illegal.
5. That it is the right of the subjects to petition the King, and all commitments and prosecutions for such petitioning are illegal.
25 6. That the raising or keeping a standing army within the Kingdom in time of peace, unless it be with consent of parliament, is against law.
7. That the subjects which are Protestants may have arms for their defence suitable to their conditions, and as allowed by law.
8. That election of members of parliament ought to be free.

30 9. That the freedom of speech, and debates or proceedings in parliament, ought not to be impeached or questioned in any court or place out of parliament.

10. That excessive bail ought not to be required, nor excessive fines imposed; nor cruel and unusual punishment inflicted.

35 11. That jurors ought to be duly impanelled and returned, and jurors which pass upon men in trials for high treason ought to be freeholders.

12. That all grants and promises of fines and forfeitures of particular persons before conviction, are illegal and void.

13. And that for redress of all grievances, and for the amending,
40 strengthening, and preserving of the laws, parliaments ought to be held frequently.

. . . To which demand of their rights they are particularly encouraged by the declaration of his Highness the Prince of Orange, as being the only means for obtaining a full redress and remedy therein.

45 Having therefore an entire confidence that his said Highness the Prince of Orange will perfect the deliverance so far advanced by him, and will still preserve them from the violation of their rights, which they have here asserted, and from all other attempts upon their religion, rights, and liberties:

50 The said Lords Spiritual and Temporal, and Commons, assembled at Westminster, do resolve, that William and Mary, Prince and Princess of Orange, be, and be declared, King and Queen of England, France, and Ireland, and the dominions thereunto belonging, to hold the Crown and royal dignity of the said Kingdom and dominions to them the said Prince
55 and Princess during their lives, and the life of the survivor of them; and that the sole and full exercise of the regal power be only in, and executed by, the said Prince of Orange, in the names of the said Prince and Princess, during their joint lives; and after their deceases, the said Crown and royal dignity of the said Kingdoms and dominions to be to the heirs of the body
60 of the said Princess, and for default of such issue to the Princess Anne of Denmark, and the heirs of her body and for default of such issue to the heirs of the body of the said Prince of Orange. And the Lords Spiritual and Temporal, and Commons, do pray the said Prince and Princess to accept the same accordingly . . . .

Bill of Rights 1689

Questions

a Which particular rights are claimed here (i) for parliament (ii) for ordinary citizens?

b What specific charges are made here about the nature of James II's rule?

* c Explain fully, from your knowledge of this period, what you understand by (i) 'cause letters to be written' (line 6) (ii) 'the pretended power of suspending laws' (line 12) (iii) 'the pretended power of dispensing with laws' (line 14).

* d   What was the historical background to the inclusion of clauses 5 and 8?

4 The Revolution and Settlement 1688–9

So James ran through the whole gamut of Stuart policy. He began with the traditional dependence on the Anglican gentry, the policy of Hyde and Danby. He flirted, as Henrietta Maria and Charles II had flirted, with the idea of imposing despotism with French support; but he was less skilful than Charles II, in extracting the maximum from the bargain and drawing back from any dangerous commitment. Then, and too obviously merely as a gambit, he revived the Indulgence policy of his brother, the alliance of Protestant and Roman Catholic dissenters against the Anglican supremacy, and again lacked Charles's wisdom in deciding when to retreat. Finally, after his desperate attempt to resuscitate the Anglican–Tory alliance had failed, he lost his head completely.

Charles I saved the Stuart monarchy by proclaiming that he died a martyr for religion, law, and property. James damned it for ever by an apparent attempt to appeal to anarchy. He departed without handing authority over to any government. He destroyed the writs summoning Parliament, and threw the Great Seal into the Thames in the vain hope of preventing one being called. He ordered the disbandment, unpaid, of the terrible army on Hounslow Heath. The navy, in which the seamen were discussing politics no less than in the Army, was ordered to sail to Tyrconnel in Ireland. Riots in London and other towns united the men of property in submission to William the Liberator. By James's absence, the loyal Sir James Bramston summed up, 'it became necessary that government should be by somebody, to avoid confusion', and to prevent 'the rabble from spoiling and robbing the nobility and wealthy . . . .

The Revolution of 1688 saw a restoration of power to the traditional ruling class, the Shire gentry, and town merchants, as well as a change of sovereigns. Borough charters were restored. The militia was returned to safe hands, and was used henceforth chiefly against any threat from the lower classes . . . .

The Revolution demonstrated the ultimate solidarity of the propertied class. Whigs and Tories disagreed sharply about whether James had abdicated or not, whether the throne should be declared vacant, whether Mary alone or William and Mary jointly should be asked to fill it, or declared to have filled it. But these differences were patched up, and the Declaration of Rights – as successful a compromise as the Elizabethan Prayer Book – simply stated both positions and left it to individuals to resolve the contradictions as they pleased. One reason for this solid front was the behaviour of James and William. The latter, so far from remaining inscrutably in the background, made it perfectly clear that he was determined to have the title of King. But a second reason for agreement was men's recollection of what had happened forty-five years earlier, when unity of the propertied classes had been broken. Like Essex and Manchester in 1644–5, Danby feared too complete a victory for either side. James's attempt to appeal to anarchy had been a warning . . . .

45 Nevertheless, if 1642–9 was not forgotten, neither were the mistakes of 1660. The Revolution Settlement set down in writing the conditions which had been tacitly assumed at the Restoration. The House of Commons resolved that, before filling the throne, it would secure the religion, laws, and liberties of the nation. The Declaration of Rights was

50 the result. Nothing could be less satisfactory as a statement of political principles. But such a statement was impossible if unity between Whigs and Tories was to be preserved. Facts were slowly causing the Tories to abandon their high-flying theories; but they could not yet be expected to admit this formality. The Declaration concentrated on removing specific

55 grievances . . . . There was still some vagueness: 'cruel and unusual punishments', 'frequent Parliaments.' But the vagueness was a price worth paying for agreement between the two parties. Any future ruler would at his peril defy those whom Parliament represented: no ruler did. The King still retained considerable powers, within the framework of the

60 rule of 'the free'. But the limits to the sovereign's power were real and recognised. William vetoed five Bills before 1696, but they all subsequently became law; after that date he used the veto no more. Anne's solitary veto in 1708 is the last in English history.

Some of the vagueness of the Declaration of Rights was cleared up by

65 later legislation. The Triennial Act (1694) provided not only that Parliaments should meet every three years but also that they should not last longer than three years. Henceforth Parliament was a necessary and continuous part of the constitution, in closer dependence on the electorate. The Act of Settlement prohibited the pleading of a royal

70 pardon to an impeachment, and so removed the last barrier to Parliamentary control of ministers.

Christopher Hill, *The Century of Revolution 1603–1714*, 1969, pp 209–10, 237–9

Questions

* *a* In what way does Hill's interpretation of James II's motives immediately prior to his flight differ from that of Mitchell (see document 1)?

  b Explain, in your own words, how James 'ran through the whole gamut of Stuart policy' (line 1).

* *c* What similarity do you detect between the motives of those who helped to bring about a Restoration in 1660 and those who engineered the Revolution in 1688 (see also section VIII)?

* *d* Show how the Bill of Rights (see document 3) 'concentrated on removing specific grievances' (lines 54 and 55).

* *e* What were 'the mistakes of 1660' (lines 45 and 46; see also section VIII)?

  f In what ways did the Settlement limit the power of the sovereign and enhance that of parliament?